THE **OTHER** SIDE OF **WAR**
WOMEN'S STORIES OF SURVIVAL & HOPE

THE OTHER SIDE OF WAR

BY ZAINAB SALBI

WOMEN'S STORIES OF SURVIVAL & HOPE

PHOTOGRAPHS BY SUSAN MEISELAS, SYLVIA PLACHY, AND LEKHA SINGH

EDITED BY LAURIE BECKLUND ▪ PREFACE BY ALICE WALKER

NATIONAL GEOGRAPHIC

WASHINGTON, D.C.

THE OTHER SIDE OF WAR

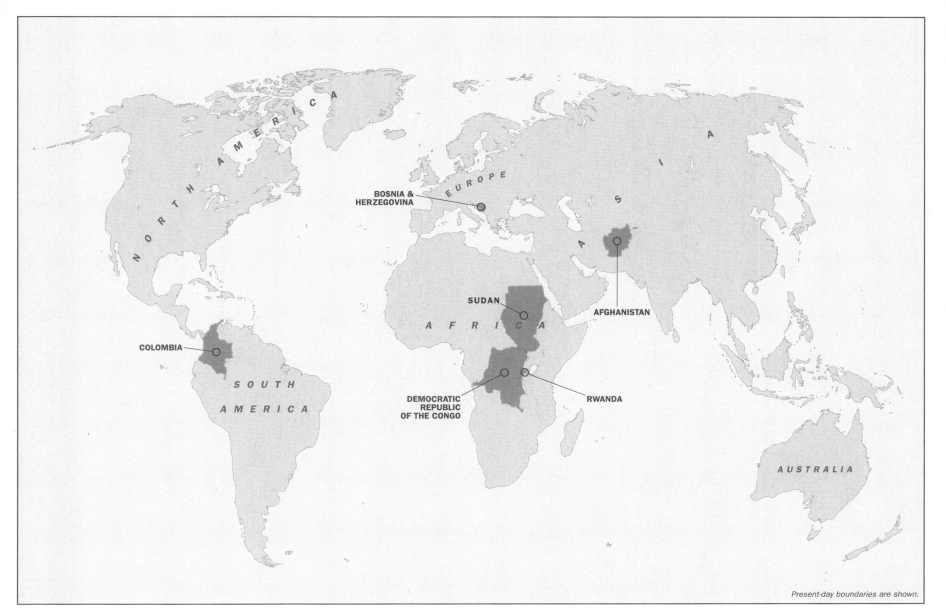

BOSNIA &
HERZEGOVINA

AFGHANISTAN

SUDAN

COLOMBIA

DEMOCRATIC
REPUBLIC
OF THE CONGO

RWANDA

NORTH AMERICA

SOUTH
AMERICA

EUROPE

AFRICA

ASIA

AUSTRALIA

Present-day boundaries are shown.

Pages 2–3: Edina, survivor of the war in Bosnia, in a village yard near Sarajevo. Women for Women International has programs in nine countries; six are highlighted above.

ABOUT WOMEN FOR WOMEN INTERNATIONAL

Founded in 1993, Women for Women International, a non-governmental organization, helps women in war-torn regions rebuild their lives by providing financial and emotional support, job skills training, rights awareness and leadership education, and access to business skills, capital, and markets. Through the program, women become confident, independent, and productive as they embrace the importance of their roles in rebuilding their families, their communities and ultimately, their nations.

Participation in a one-year program launches women on a journey from victim to survivor to active citizen. Women begin in the sponsorship program where direct financial aid from a sponsor helps them deal with the immediate effects of war and conflict such as lack of food, water, medicine, and other necessities. Exchanging letters with sponsors provides women with an emotional lifeline and a chance to tell their stories—maybe for the first time. As their situations begin to stabilize, women in the program begin building a foundation for their lives as survivors.

While receiving sponsorship support, women participate in the Renewing Women's Life Skills (ReneWLS) Program that provides them with rights awareness, leadership education, and vocational and technical skills training. Women build upon existing skills and learn new ones to regain their strength, stability, and stature.

Women for Women International believes that establishing a means to earn a sustainable living is critical to being fully active in the life of a family, community, and country. To help women transform their skills into financial independence, the program offers job skills training so the women can be self-employed or find other ways to generate income in the future.

Building on the skills training, the program offers business-development services designed to help women start and manage their own microenterprises. Women for Women International provides access to capital and operates microcredit programs in selected countries. The program helps women access markets by facilitating product sales and provides expertise in product design, production assistance, and business basics. Women also receive help in setting up production facilities, cooperatives, and stores that sell goods that women produce.

The organization is currently working in Afghanistan, Bosnia and Herzegovina, Colombia, Democratic Republic of the Congo, Iraq, Kosovo, Nigeria, Rwanda, and Sudan.

To help change the lives of women survivors of war, visit www.womenforwomen.org.

Judithe Registre (opposite) is the country director for Sudan and former country director for the Democratic Republic of the Congo for Women for Women International.

PREFACE

What is happening
in Africa
(& elsewhere)
is because
the men
did not listen
to the women
& the women
did not listen
to the women
either
& because
the people did not listen
to each other
& themselves
& because
nobody listened
to the children
&
the poets.
—*Alice Walker*

...This is the way
The world
Ends
This is the way
The world
Ends
This is the way
The world
Ends
Not with
A bang
But a
Whimper.
—*T.S. Eliot*
from *The Hollow Men*

As I write, I am sitting in a garden in a country that does not appear, to an outsider, to be at war. It is a "third world" or "developing" country, and as elsewhere the gap between haves and have-nots is rapidly widening. Many of the poorest people, whose lives have been shattered by a war that everyone says is over in the southern regions, pass through the small towns that dot the countryside, on their way to the United States, desperately looking for work. They have only the clothes they are wearing; their faces are drawn; no one smiles. We understand, seeing these faces, that though this war "in the southern regions" may be over for everyone else, it will never be over for them.

On the roads there are few vehicles, and I notice, not for the first time, that almost all the drivers in the cars and trucks, are men. An ill omen, I think, for the society at large, because it speaks to an ingrained gender inequality that drastically curtails the mobility and involvement in life of women and girls and will undoubtedly undermine any dream of progress and societal stability. After all, how can a society flourish, a country attain democracy and health, children grow into intelligent beings, sensitive to the needs of an ever more fragile and endangered planet, if half its people are kept out of the driver's seat? How can a world right itself and find its true direction, if only men are taught to steer the vehicle that would take it there? Alas, the roads resemble only too closely the country's political and spiritual leadership, all of it masculine.

In this garden, with its bougainvillea, its white butterflies, and red ginger, I have eaten a breakfast of oatmeal and an egg. I have savored the taste of food in my mouth, the sun on my face, the security of knowing it is not likely that someone will arrive with machetes and guns to smash me and my computer, trash my dwelling, and commit other atrocities that have traditionally left women too stunned and ashamed to speak of them. I mention the garden, the flowers, the butterflies, the oatmeal, and the egg because it is essential to remember what so many in the world, especially women, are losing to war. The simplest necessities and pleasures: a flower, an egg, a child's smile, a partner's caress, sun on our faces, clean water to drink, an unbroken night's rest, a private moment to lend wings to our dreams: These things are our birthright. As are: a place of our own, sufficient food,

a sound education, freedom from assault, excellent medical attention. All these things are within reach, costing far less than the massively overproduced weapons that are stockpiled, or horribly in use, around the world. It is our duty to demand these things, not just for ourselves, but for everyone on this small planet.

When you read this book, which is crucial for every person who wants a future to read, you may weep. There is no shame in this. And also, your tears may fall on the inside, and they may not come when you expect them. But they will come, if you care at all about the fate of humanity. When you read this book, you will be astounded at how far we have fallen, as a species, from what we assumed was our innate integrity, dignity, and decency as human beings. How driven we have become by a self-hatred that has set us, pitilessly, against ourselves. Because, in fact, there is no "other" anywhere. It is always us, and only us, that we wound, whenever we harm another. There is no way to be separate from the rest of creation; we indulge the fantasy of being separate to our peril, which brings us to that which truly leaves us speechless and gasping at its insatiable nature: human greed. For it is the greed of humans and our addiction to war as a method of resolving conflict that spreads this carnage and suffering. We humans are forgetting our very essence as divine beings. It is a terrifying state of affairs.

What are we becoming? How hard is it to look?

Who can imagine 800,000 people being hacked to death with machetes in the span of four months? That number means more people than the population of most cities. Who can truly grasp the horror of 500,000 women and girls being raped, many of them mutilated or murdered, during this same period? Who can fathom the violation of infants, their tiny bodies ripped apart and left bleeding in the street; and the repeated raping of women until there is no lining left between vagina and intestines? Who can imagine one's neighbor joining with other men to destroy one's dwelling, shoot one's children, rape, and deliberately impregnate all females that can be found so that the "enemy" will live perpetually inside the doomed community? What has happened inside a person that commits these crimes? What has happened to a world that, out of confusion, disbelief, and fear, ignores them? Will our disbelief, confusion, and fear only be activated toward change when we hear the sound of killers at our own door?

We must rouse ourselves, awaken to our predicament, as humans; as people who know there is goodness in all of us. Women, in their capacity as nurturers and sustainers of the young continue to exhibit a lot of human goodness and for that reason alone, should be honored and protected.

How can the world live without war? Someone must know. Is it possible that women have always known? What is the deepest reason women have been forced into their so often fatal silence? Is it because women are always wanting peace, and men have learned to enjoy war? How does one begin to account for women's low status, globally, given the fact that it is through them that everything human is produced?

I remember years ago being asked by a young Iraqi woman (through a mutual friend), if I would be an honorary founding member of Women for Women International, an organization she was forming. When I read her proposal: to help women who have survived war by offering friendship, financial assistance, and training, I knew at once it was the sensible, and moral, thing to do. More than a decade later Zainab Salbi's organization has helped countless women in diverse countries to gain not only a livelihood and, in some instances, a first ever autonomy, but a basic sense of self they did not have before the calamity of war befell them. It is this transformation, this rise of the phoenix from the ashes, that offers that most invaluable and much prayed for spiritual gift, the inspiration of hope.

It is out of Zainab Salbi's work directly with women who have (barely) survived war that this book comes. This is not just another book. It is a document women (and men who respect women) must use to figure out how we can survive, intact, as the manifestation of the healthy and autonomous feminine that is essential to bringing the Earth back to balance. In an all masculine world, which many men assume they want and presume they can have, men would die of longing.

To change the world for the better, to make it safe for the feminine, which is to make it safe for everyone, women must work together. Even if we do not like each other, we must work together anyway, as impersonal friends who face a common danger. When we work together, the entire society benefits. That is what the work of Women for Women International demonstrates. That yes, we may be marginalized and seemingly without resources, but out of the deep feminine values of caring, compassion, and courage we bring whatever we have to the common table of woman. There we meet our sisters. They have brought all that they have as well. We sit: Sometimes the table is our bare Mother Earth. We talk, we strategize, we plan. We help each other. We never forget what war has taught us. Never again will we be resigned to illiteracy, weakness, and powerlessness, forced to let selfish men, whether fathers, brothers, lovers, husbands, or friends lead us into ever darkening ignorance and servitude.

We have had enough. We insist on acquiring knowledge for ourselves and for our daughters, having learned the hardest ways possible that ignorance and peace cannot coexist. We know we can create a better way of living than any of the societies—whether democracies or dictatorships—that have silenced us and used our bodies and minds without reverence or gratitude.

We have learned all we need to know of leadership that insults, marginalizes, and ignores us. We will have no more of it, of this we are certain. Knowing this, we understand something very important: We, having been so nearly destroyed, can use what we learned from our destruction to start the world again.

And so may it be.

—*Alice Walker*

INTRODUCTION

How can we talk about war without talking about its colors? The colors of fire and blood, the color of earth as it explodes in our face? In that moment when a bomb falls or a missile lands, there comes a light so bright, it penetrates every crevice of whatever refuge you hoped might keep you safe. You are completely exposed by this impossible brightness, utterly vulnerable.

How can we talk about war without talking about its sounds? War is not just gunfire or explosions, but a dissonant concert: a flock of birds screeching in the night, a stranger breathing in your ear, the sound of your child pleading. Even worse, it is silence of children so terrorized they do not scream, or the silence of your own guilty prayer of thanks that it was not your children who died. War, says a friend of mine, is not about sound at all, but about silence. The silence of humanity.

How can we talk about war without talking about fear? War, as a Bosnian woman named Samija once wrote, took the "I" in "me." Ever since I read her description, I have thought about this other side of war, where a woman struggles to maintain her *self* even as the ground under her feet is dissolving in a sea of fear and suspicion. A Palestinian woman defined this fear for me as the feeling of being in a perpetual process of dying. "There are times in which I feel I've died ten times a day," she said, recalling soldiers who patrolled her neighborhood day and night, punctuating their rounds with gunfire. "But there is only one life, and there should be only one death."

A century ago, 90 percent of war casualties were male soldiers. There have been 250 major conflicts since World War II with 23 million acknowledged casualties. Today, an estimated 90 percent of casualties are civilians, and 75 percent of these are estimated to be women and children. Research shows that women are more likely to be displaced as a result of war, more likely to be sole providers of children and the elderly, and more likely to die of disease caused by the lack of sanitation wars create. In wars where rape and mutilation of women have been epidemic, as in the case of Bosnia and Herzegovina, Rwanda, Sudan, and the Democratic Republic of the Congo, countless women live with physically and emotionally debilitating war wounds. When a man is injured in war, he is a hero. But when a woman is raped or mutilated because of rape, she is more likely hidden, an object of shame.

Politicians, analysts, and sometimes journalists adopt dispassionate, seemingly objective, ways of discussing wars in terms of politics, tactics, and numbers of weapons, dollars, and casualties expended. Satellites peer down with nonhuman eyes on our perceived enemies, guiding missiles toward unseen targets. We may speak of "collateral damage," but do so typically in abstract terms, with the tacit understanding that it is a necessary evil not to be examined too closely, lest the colors, the sounds, and the silences be revealed.

If we are to understand war fully, we need to understand not only what happens on the front lines, but what happens on the back lines as well, where women are in charge of keeping *life* going. This book is meant to go beyond the bullets, the battles, and the politics to present nuanced views of war held by the women who have lived through it. The stories they tell are of incredible loss and cruelty, but they reveal an equally incredible degree of courage and creativity that shows women in their full agency, not merely as victims.

War often enters homes through the kitchen door. Women sense war's onset early, as they deal with shortages of food, and the closing of schools, and often their own reduced freedoms.

Where oppression against women is growing, oppression of society at large is likely at hand. For our own benefit, we must acknowledge

Zainab Salbi interviewing women in Sudan.

this clear pattern: What happens to women is often an indicator of what is to come for the rest of the society, be it war or peace, economic marginalization or economic development, illiteracy or education, stagnation or progress.

One need only to look at recent history. Afghanistan's Taliban started with the easiest target in sight: women. First women were to be protected, then secluded, then banned from being educated or receiving medical attention. To the extent the world noticed, this was seen as "just" more oppression of women in an already oppressive culture. In Rwanda, changes in the status of women also served as a precursor to conflict. Derogatory remarks about Tutsi women and ways in which they should be raped were among the first remarks the *Interahamwe—*

15

the extremist Hutu militia—made in radio announcements and public speeches impelling genocide.

In Iraq, women were the first group to be targeted for kidnapping after the fall of Saddam Hussein. Women were abducted from the streets, from their schools, from their jobs, and even from their homes. But their cries fell on deaf ears: The increasingly precarious status of women was seen as a secondary issue, a distraction from the bigger political debates. Soon, every politician, business person, professional, Iraqi and foreigner alike became vulnerable to kidnapping. This issue has become big enough to actually impede development efforts in the country.

Women's bodies are treated as part of the battlefield. Consider the story of Ajsa, the first survivor of rape camps in Bosnia and Herzegovina I met during my first trip to the region. In the camps, women were repeatedly gang raped and told they "deserved" to be raped because they were Muslims. "This is to avenge what the Turks did to our grandfathers," their rapists said. What the men didn't mention was that they were avenging acts that happened hundreds of years ago. This was my first exposure to the ways in which rape is used to achieve political and social goals, from the destruction of the social fabric of the society, to avenging historical acts, to political propaganda.

Some 20,000 women like Ajsa were raped in such camps. Many never made it to camps at all; girls as young as four were raped in the mountains, in their homes, and in the midst of their villages and towns. Fathers were ordered to rape daughters and executed when they refused. One woman told me, soldiers had held her son's eyes open to force him to witness her rape.

Through it all, the humanity of each woman, each person, is ignored. Ignored, too, is the quality of daily life that follows for such women, who will never be free of the excruciating memories of their attacks, nor the ongoing pain and embarrassment of fistula, mutilation, or HIV infections that relegate so many so needlessly to lives of outcasts, beggars, or prostitutes. Yet, when war ends, women are the first to pick up the pieces. Where there is no marketplace, they go door to door. When homes are destroyed, mothers and daughters haul stones to rebuild or plow fields together.

Through their stories, women help us understand the real costs of war, the interruption to the basic commerce of daily living, the way it upends families and downsizes even the most modest dreams. Through their stories, we also learn how to rebuild a country, a community, and a family.

Perhaps it is time to listen. No one taught me more about the power of telling a story than Nabito, a widow and mother of 12 from a small village in eastern Congo. Before I met her, Nabito had been raped by eight men, who forced her sons to participate in restraining her. Soldiers ordered one of her sons to rape her; when he refused, they shot him. Nabito's daughters were raped near their mother. As she told me her story, Nabito's forearm fluttered out of control, so badly broken by her attackers that it almost appeared as if she had an extra elbow.

When I asked Nabito what I should do with her story, which she had never told anybody before, she looked at me and said: "If I could tell the world about what happened to me and that would help prevent other women from facing similar crimes, I would, but I can't," she said. "You go ahead and tell the world about my story just not the neighbors." A year later, Nabito was featured on the Oprah Winfrey Show talking to the whole world about what happened to her. Change happens because women like Nabito decide to talk and not take their silence to their death. Rape laws were changed in Rwanda because women talked. Rape was prosecuted as a war crime by the International Criminal Tribunal first for Rwanda and then for the former Yugoslavia because Rwandan, Bosnian, and Croatian women talked.

Like war itself, this book is a mosaic, a mixture of intimate stories and pictures as told by the women survivors of war and as captured by three remarkable women photographers in six very different conflict and post-conflict countries: Bosnia and Herzegovina, the Democratic Republic of the Congo, Colombia, Sudan, Afghanistan, and Rwanda. Perhaps by understanding this other side of war, we will think twice before engaging in facile discussions of numbers and statistics that distance the topic from its full human truth. This book is about women and what they see and say about war, and how they survived it.

Women often speak about war not as a series of battles, but as a journey that often begins with abrupt displacement from all that is familiar. The reasons that force people out of their homes vary from one place to another, but the stories women tell of their journeys are remarkably similar regardless of a woman's social standing, ethnicity, or level of education.

Always, it seems, they speak of running into darkness. It is not just a physical darkness they flee, but the safety of home into a future of loneliness and abject fear. Often there is no warning of the violence to come. One young Congolese newlywed you will meet in this book talks about losing her "real" life in the few seconds that elapsed between the time it took her to remove her baby's dirty diaper and to put on a clean one. That was when the men with the machetes came, and she ran into the forest with her baby, naked and slippery, in her arms. She fell. They slid. When she woke up, it was in a hospital without hands.

"We had to escape in the middle of the night," an Iraqi woman told me in tears. "We had to run in the midst of a very dark forest. We could not see anything. I couldn't see who was in front of me and who was behind me. I couldn't see where I was heading. All I knew is what I was escaping from…. My mother could not keep up with the others, so I went back for her. She told me to run and save my soul…but I couldn't. I held her hand and dragged her behind me. Nothing mattered to me at that point but to save my mother and run to the unknown."

The story of one woman's flight was told to our staff in Sarajevo by her husband, a frail old man who came to register his wife for our program. One of our Sarajevo staff members explained that our policy didn't allow anyone except the woman herself. Tears came into his eyes. He sat down and took off the traditional beret many Bosnian men wear. "The only reason I am here is because my wife is sick and could not make it out of her bed today," he explained. And he started telling us how, when they learned soldiers were headed for their village after pillaging villages before it, the two had run into the mountains at night, joining other villagers who were also trying to flee. While fleeing, he fell and broke his glasses, without which he could not see. "Go ahead," he told her. "Save your life. Run," he repeated. "But my wife came back to get me and carried me on her back," he said. "I owe her my life, and I will do anything to help her be happy."

These flights from danger can last days, months, or years. There is rarely transportation—or even water. Women just walk and walk, often with their children. Sometimes they find other women who open their homes to them. Often, they face new dangers as they go. They eat whatever they can find along the way. When they sleep, under a tree, or in a marsh, or in a shed, or in the open desert, they risk abduction and rape. One Sudanese mother of two children we meet in this book walked for a month with 40 other women. The young women among them were raped by soldiers, and their babies were attacked by lions.

Women and children make up 80 percent of refugees worldwide. Often, women sit in camps while children play around them, inventing games out of nothing. Sometimes the children cry out for attention, but the mothers and grandmothers still do not move. With dazed eyes, many clutch plastic bags containing photos or reminders of lives otherwise erased. "Find someone else to help," one widowed Kosovar woman advised me. "I am too helpless to be helped."

In these camps, survivors become numbers in food lines. There is no privacy in a refugee camp—you no longer have a door you can close, a garden to escape to, or a routine you can call your own. Your home is a tent made up of fabric tricked by winds into revealing your every move. You are utterly accessible to anybody who wants to talk with you, interview you, take your picture, or expose your vulnerability. You no longer have your support network of family and friends. In a refugee camp, you suffer all alone in public. Some refugee camps in Croatia that hosted Bosnian refugees kept rape victims in a separate section topped with a sign reading RAPE VICTIMS to facilitate interviews. The same thing happened again in refugee camps in Albania and Macedonia for Kosovar refugees.

In Pakistan, where there were hundreds of camps for Afghan refugees at the time of the Taliban, some toilets were a 15-minute walk from living areas. Because Afghan culture does not typically permit a woman to walk alone, women would have to schedule group trips, often just one a day, to use the toilet. Today, in places like Darfur, when Sudanese women need to venture out for firewood or water, they are open to attacks, kidnapping, or rape. Even inside the camps, women are vulnerable to violence, both from men who live there and, despite guidelines against it, from the very United Nations soldiers who have been sent to protect them, as in the case of the Democratic Republic of the Congo.

And refugees who make it to these camps are the lucky ones. Within eyeshot of many official refugee camps, where residents are fed and housed, lie unofficial squatter settlements where refugees get nothing. I met an Afghan woman who had quilted a tent out of pieces of plastic, sheets, newspapers, and bits of refuse because she was refused admittance to a refugee camp whose internal politics were dominated by an opposing tribe. "I had a house once, you know," she told me with intense eyes. "Every time I go out begging, I pray to God to take my soul so I may be spared this humiliation."

Just when I find myself haunted by some new horror of war, stories of the durability of the human spirit revive me. In an Albanian refugee camp in Kosova, I remember the bravery of one family I met, who stopped to pick up three distraught girls who had been dumped, naked and vulnerable, in the middle of a street, after having been raped by soldiers in the mountains. This family was fleeing for their own lives, but they stopped to save the girls and clothe them, claiming them as their own until they could be reunited with their families.

Historically, men have shaped the discussions, not only of war, but of peace and reconstruction as well. They assume control of the public sphere, negotiating new constitutions and planning for physical and economic reconstruction. Women, meanwhile, are left to deal with narrowly defined "women's" issues or retreat to their prewar roles, as Rosie the Riveter was expected to do in the United States after World War II—simply hand in her toolbox and return to the kitchen so soldiers returning from war could have their jobs back. Recent examples can be found in Bosnia and Herzegovina, Kosovo, and Iraq.

This pattern has been explained in different ways: Men have the need to resume their traditional positions, the vast majority of politicians are men, and they have no awareness of the value women bring to the table; and, perhaps the worst explanation, which simply dismisses the trend as an entrenched cultural issue. Whatever the reason, women's input is rarely included when it comes to questions of building economies, political structures, and social change. Their most basic rights—the right to mobility, to equity in marriage and property and education—are negotiated away to conservative establishments in exchange for what are seen as stepping-stones toward some grander concept of nation-building.

Not only are women the majority of postwar populations (in postgenocide Rwanda, it was estimated that 70 percent were women, but they also represent a critical mass when it comes to rebuilding economies, school systems, civil societies, and democracies. Sustainable peace and economies are not sustainable at all if women are not a critical part of making them happen. A Rwandan senator told me that no economy could be built, and no society rebuilt, without taking into account its critical mass. "And in postwar," she said, "it is women."

Occasionally war so upends societal norms that a window of opportunity opens, and women find ways to renegotiate their roles and express their views on social, economic, and political issues. Rwanda presents one of the most successful examples of full incorporation of women in solving societal problems and rebuilding the country. When it became known that the genocide had left 500,000 orphaned children and only a handful of orphanages, Rwandan women organized to launch an adoption campaign within the country. The success of this and other campaigns proved that women were both powerful and vital to the resolution of national issues. Today, almost 50 percent of the Rwandan Parliament is women, the highest percentage of representation of women in such bodies worldwide.

The Rwandan leadership has responded with sustained commitment to the advancement of women and elevation of their status.

Through the women featured in this book and the countless others whom I have been privileged to meet and work with, I have learned the meaning of strength and resilience, the power of the concept "hope," and the importance of women's roles in keeping their families alive and their societies intact.

I met Beatrice in a two-room mud hut she built with the help of other women survivors of a massacre in a Rwandan church. "I remember machetes flying around right and left as they cut people in every part of their bodies," she said. "I woke up many hours later to see that I was still alive. On top of me were the bodies of my seven children." With a look on her face that revealed her ongoing struggle to reconcile the past with the present, she spoke of how she had run into the night hoping to find a place to hide. Instead, she was captured and raped, hacked on the neck with a machete, and left, once again, for dead.

But Beatrice found a new "I" in herself. She bore the child of her rapist and adopted five children orphaned by the genocide. She has empowered a family and helped restore a community. Yet, who measures her economic contribution? Who gives medals of valor to women like her?

Women like Beatrice chose to live and move beyond tragedy that could have so easily consumed them. They are resilient, powerful women who are also social entrepreneurs, heads of households, and economic pillars of their communities. In this book, you will meet women with headscarves and women with bare legs, women who see themselves as religious and women who see themselves as secular. Some are educated, and some are illiterate. Some want paid jobs, and some want only to raise their children in safety. They are victims and survivors. But these things do not define them. Their stories tell us about war in close-up, profoundly human terms. Their wisdom about war is deep because their experience spans the emotional and the pragmatic elements of survival.

As Rumi, my favorite Sufi poet of the 13th century wrote, "between the worlds of right-doing and wrong-doing, there is a field; I will meet you there." I think in today's world there is a field between the worlds of war and peace, and women are meeting there. I am honored to introduce them to you.

—*Zainab Salbi*

BOSNIA & HERZEGOVINA

NEXT TIME WE HAVE A WAR,

I WILL BE THE FIRST ONE TO PICK UP A WEAPON

AND FIGHT. I NO LONGER TRUST ANYONE

TO PROTECT US.

—A BOSNIAN WOMAN

Photographs by Sylvia Plachy

TERROR AT THE CROSSROADS

It was the war that gave the world the terms "ethnic cleansing" and "rape camps." The year was 1992. The mountains of eastern Bosnia and Herzegovina were under threat of attack from Serbian nationalists as the former socialist nation of Yugoslavia was falling apart. The United Nations declared the town of Srebrenica a "safe haven" for Bosnians, who surrendered their weapons in exchange for protection. Two years later, Serbian soldiers and police attacked, overwhelming the 400 lightly armed Dutch UN peacekeepers. Serbian soldiers stole UN helmets and vehicles, took 14 peacekeepers hostage, and loaded 25,000 Bosnian women and children onto buses for a journey over treacherous roads into camps in the Serbian-controlled Bosnian territory. Thousands of men and boys tried to flee through the mountains; many were never seen again.

Serb forces agreed to return the peacekeepers in exchange for 5,000 residents of Srebrenica who had taken refuge in a UN compound nearby. The slaughter began after the peacekeepers departed. In the end, Serb forces massacred nearly 8,000 Bosnian boys and men—the worst massacre in Europe since World War II. Only later did the International Criminal Tribunal for the Former Yugoslavia rule it genocide; in the eyes of many, Srebrenica stands for the failure of the international community to protect civilians during war.

The Srebrenica crimes are the most horrifying example of "ethnic cleansing" that pervaded Bosnia and Herzegovina's four years of war. The euphemism, translated from Serbo-Croatian, would one day be used worldwide to apply to the destructive power of ethnic nationalism.

Bosnia and Herzegovina emerged from World War II as one of six republics of the nation of Yugoslavia. But unlike the other five—Slovenia, Croatia, Serbia, Montenegro, and Macedonia—Bosnia and Herzegovina had no ethnic majority. The republic was a mix of Bosnian Muslims (also known as Bosniaks), Catholic Croats, Orthodox Serbs, and smaller Jewish and Hungarian communities. The three major groups shared racial, linguistic, and cultural heritages and had lived together in relative peace; at least a third of Bosnia and Herzegovina's marriages crossed ethnic lines. Most people identified themselves as Bosnians first and secondarily as members of ethnic groups.

When Yugoslavian leader Josip Broz Tito died in 1980, the nation faced economic decline and political instability, and the multinational

Previous pages: Graffiti in Sarajevo.

balance disintegrated. Slobodan Milosevic, a Serbian Communist leader, emerged as president, stirring Serb nationalism in hopes of gaining territory to create a Greater Serbia and alienating other Yugoslav republics. The first republic to secede—peacefully—from Yugoslavia was Slovenia. Croatia voted to secede in 1991, only to face a brutal response by Milosevic. Bosnian Croats and Bosniaks followed suit in 1992, calling for a referendum for Bosnian independence.

Milosevic attempted to gain support for his nationalist aims by spreading fear among Bosnian Serbs and hate-filled propaganda that painted Bosniaks as dangerous fundamentalists. Nearly a million Yugoslavs had died at the hands of fellow citizens in World War II, and Milosevic used war stories of mass killings of Serbs and other groups carried out by Croatian fascists as propaganda to fuel hatred, ignoring killing by Serbs during the same period.

After Bosnia and Herzegovina was officially declared independent, Bosniaks, Croats, and Serbs each organized armies and paramilitary groups. Bosniak and Croat forces fought together against Serbs and eventually turned on each other as Croats tried to claim parts of western and southern Bosnia and Herzegovina. While not all Serbs succumbed

to Milosevic's rhetoric, and all sides have had their share of war crimes, Serb nationalism was the driving force behind the war's exceptional ethnic brutality.

Bosnian Serbs staged a 43-month siege of Sarajevo, the second longest siege in modern history. Those trapped inside the city paid bitterly for resisting Serbian nationalism and holding fast to the memory of a multiethnic Sarajevo. Before the war, Catholic and Orthodox churches sat across the street from mosques and synagogues in the artistic and cultural center of Bosnia and Herzegovina, renowned for its outstanding symphony, libraries, art galleries, and museums. The siege made prisoners out of ordinary people. Food and medicine were scarce. A tunnel out of the war zone dug by volunteers with picks and shovels brought desperately needed supplies into the city. Residents of Sarajevo suffered through three freezing winters, holed up in their homes without heat or electricity to escape the heavy shelling of the snipers and gunners ringing the city. In desperation, they created makeshift stoves, burning furniture, shoes, and books in order to survive.

The death of one couple, later dubbed "Romeo and Juliet," came to symbolize the war's tragedy to many Bosnians and to the world. Serb Bosko Brkic and his childhood sweetheart, Bosniak Admira Ismic, died in each other's arms, shot by sniper fire as they crossed the city's most dangerous bridge in the hopes of fleeing to a better life.

The siege of Sarajevo was not only about killing. It was an attempt to destroy the city's cultural and historic identity. The city library burned for three days as Serbian army snipers targeted the firemen who tried to save the building. Hundreds of mosques and churches were burned to the ground. Yet acts of defiance revealed the determination of many Bosnians to retain normalcy in the midst of chaos and resist the destruction of their heritage. The staff of the National Museum, one of the few cultural institutions to survive the war, stood guard at night to protect the building. Musicians held concerts in burned-out libraries; people used shrapnel to make art, crafting decorative vases out of empty shells.

Bosnians in rural areas suffered tremendously. Serbian forces drove nearly half of the country's population, or two million people, out of their homes, destroying entire villages and burning thousands of houses to the ground. The Serbian military enslaved, raped, and tortured at least 20,000 women, some in the 16 rape camps they constructed for that purpose. Women were forcibly impregnated and held in the camps until late stages of pregnancy, then were required to leave with no provisions or homes to return to. The children resulting from rape were viewed by Serbs as "clean and purified."

The war finally ended with the signing of the Dayton Peace Agreement on November 21, 1995, in Dayton, Ohio, after previous peace plans had failed. The agreement divided the country into a joint Bosniak/Croat Federation of Bosnia and Herzegovina and a Bosnian Serb-led Republika Srpska. The UN deployed 60,000 peacekeepers to the country. In an act seen as a betrayal by survivors of the massacre, the agreement turned Srebrenica over to the "Serbian Republic."

International aid initially poured into Bosnia and Herzegovina amidst criticism that the international community had failed to adequately respond while the war's atrocities were at their height. More than ten years later, as the hearts and pocketbooks of the world shifted to new hotspots, the hardships of war are not yet over.

Women have shouldered much of the burden of reconstruction. Approximately 175,000 people, mostly men, are thought to have died in the war. Women, many widowed or supporting injured husbands, were left to contend with the shock of poverty and deprivation in a country that had once been primarily middle class. The pressure by international donors to continue Bosnia and Herzegovina's prewar transition from a state-run to a market economy has added to the challenges of rebuilding the country's systems and institutions.

Women's new enemy is poverty. An estimated 70 percent of the population experiences some measure of poverty—whether lack of food, work, or medical care. The formal unemployment rate is 44 percent, at least 60 percent of whom are women. When jobs are available, classified ads often seek women "of an appealing look, under the age of 35."

Throughout Bosnia and Herzegovina, women have mobilized to take rebuilding into their own hands. The republic did not have a strong women's movement before the war, but women's organizations have sprung up. They counsel survivors of violence, run microcredit programs, and promote women in politics. In Busovaca, a town in central Bosnia and Herzegovina greatly damaged by the war, women of diverse backgrounds are working together to identify and solve problems in their communities. "If it could work in Busovaca," says Sanja, a community leader, "it could work anywhere."

The International Criminal Tribunal for the former Yugoslavia (ICTY), following a precedent set by the ICT for Rwanda, prosecuted rape as a crime against humanity. Women all over the world joined forces with the Bosnian women to applaud their courage in breaking the silence and publicly testifying about the atrocities that had been committed against them. Bosnian women are known for this historic break with the unspoken covenant that pressed them into accepting these crimes in silence. Their determination inspired a major shift, bringing atrocities against women to the public fore. International women activists successfully lobbied to change international law and enact the Law of Bosnia and Herzegovina on Gender Equality on May 21, 2003, which protects equal rights for men and women and prohibits discrimination and public and private violence on the grounds of gender.

Due to the divisions created by the Dayton Peace Agreement in some areas outside of Sarajevo, members of different ethnic groups have separate schools and medical services. Divisions remain deep. Yet, one finds signs of hope, even in Srebrenica, where some Bosniak families have returned to their homes and helped revive—amid the abandoned houses and family graves—a prewar tradition to see who can grow the most beautiful garden. Even in Mostar, where the international community has stepped in and rebuilt an ancient bridge.

Milka, a raspberry
and dairy farmer, with sons.

WHEN I THINK ABOUT A CROSSROAD IN MY LIFE, IT WAS DURING THIS AWFUL WAR.

WE BUILT A HOUSE BEFORE THE WAR, AND IT WAS FILLED WITH LAUGHTER

AND HAPPINESS.... THE WAR STARTED IN 1992.... IT MADE GREAT DAMAGE

TO THE ECONOMY AND TRADE, AND DESTROYED OUR PEACE. WE WERE NOT LIVING DURING

THESE FOUR YEARS. WE WERE SURVIVING. WE DIDN'T HAVE ANYTHING.

THEY WANTED TO STOP US EVEN THE LIGHT AND THE AIR. THEY WANTED TO DESTROY

OUR CULTURE AS A WHOLE PEOPLE AND MAKE GREAT SERBIA STAND ON

THE SOIL FULL OF THE BLOOD OF OUR INNOCENT CHILDREN....

WE HAVE BITTER IN OUR MOUTH, BUT WE KNOW WE HAVE TO GO ON

BECAUSE OF OUR CHILDREN.

—SABIRA

MY DAUGHTERS
GIVE ME HAPPINESS.
I LIVE FOR THEM—
THEY ARE KEEPING
ME ALIVE.

—ZIKRETA
from Busovaca

Zikreta and her daughters.

FAMILY BUSINESS

*Lucija, second from left,
with her family in Busovaca shows off a
young chicken. Her first business
venture was raising chickens.
Now she sells thousands of jars of jams
and organic red pepper chutney.
Her business doubles annually,
allowing her to hire
family, friends, and villagers.
She suspects that women's laughter adds
flavor to her condiments.*

WE EVEN HIRED ONE ENTIRE VILLAGE TO PICK ROSE HIP

OR US TO MAKE OUR JAM.... IT IS A GOOD FEELING TO PROVIDE JOBS FOR OTHER PEOPLE.—LUCIJA

MILK FOR MANY

Cows are like family members for many Bosnians like Fata (right). They provide milk for children and cheese to sell. So many cows fled, starved, or were slaughtered during the war that cows had to be imported when it was over.

FROM ASHES

When Fata and her daughter-in-law, Senida (left), returned home after the war, they found only ashes. They moved into the basement, survived by growing potatoes, and began rebuilding. "We were the only ones strong enough to make something for our family," Fata said.

REMEMBERING

"My husband was away digging trenches that night…
then knocking on our door started,
and we heard voices, which asked us to open the door,"
says Safeta (at right and on the following pages),
as she relates the horrors of abduction
and rape by soldiers and some of her own neighbors.
"They did not even wear any masks."

I SUFFERED, BUT THINGS THAT DON'T KILL YOU

MAKE YOU STRONGER. HOW COULD I POSSIBLY SHOW MY CHILDREN THE RIGHT PATH IN LIFE...

...IF I LET LIFE BREAK ME DOWN?—SAFETA

SAFETA

Safeta and her family are marginalized even by postwar Bosnian standards. Her husband finds seasonal jobs when possible. Safeta cleans homes and picks wild berries to sell. They fear the onset of winter.

Now 36, she remembers a time when she was young and in love and so beautiful her husband was nervous about the looks other men gave her. When she became pregnant, she remembers thinking, her life was "perfect." Then Serbian forces attacked Bosniak settlements, burning and looting homes in a town where Catholics and Muslims and a small Serbian Orthodox population had long lived as neighbors. Many Bosniaks fled or were forced out. Her husband was taken to a concentration camp. "People who were our neighbors one day became the enemy the next day," says Safeta, who gave birth while he was gone. "Busovaca became the ghetto for Bosniaks."

Her husband was eventually released from prison, but was required to do forced labor 48 hours at a time. He was away digging ditches the night militants banged on their door and threatened to kill her baby if she screamed. She recognized some of the men as neighbors and begged for mercy, but they marched her off to an abandoned house and raped her repeatedly. She still remembers the voice of the man who wore a mask. No need to kill her, he told the others when they were done. She will kill herself.

But she didn't. Instead, she camped out for days at the office of the United Nations High Commissioner for Refugees, successfully pleading for safe passage for her family to a free territory. After the war ended, she and her husband returned to Busovaca only to find their home in ashes. Safeta was invited to testify against her attackers at a war crimes tribunal in The Hague, but no one could provide her family asylum afterward, so she refused.

Today, the modest home she shares with her husband and two sons exudes warmth and order. "I am a happy and cheerful woman because I have my family alive and well," she says. Yet, whenever she hears the voices of men outside, she goes to her window.

"I follow with my eyes men who are passing by," she says defiantly. "In case it is one of them, I want them to see that I am still alive, that they did not kill me, neither body nor soul, nor will they ever be able to do it."

I DO NOT HAVE TO TALK MUCH

ABOUT SREBRENICA. THE WHOLE WORLD

KNOWS THE TRUTH ABOUT SREBRENICA....

IN ONE NIGHT ENTIRE FAMILIES

FROM MY VILLAGE—FATHERS, SONS, HUSBANDS,

BROTHERS—DISAPPEARED. WOMEN WERE

DYING OF SADNESS AND HELPLESSNESS.

WE WERE EXPELLED FROM OUR HOMES,

AND THEY WERE KILLING US JUST BECAUSE WE

BELONGED TO ANOTHER RELIGION.

—ZEJNEBA
from Bratunac

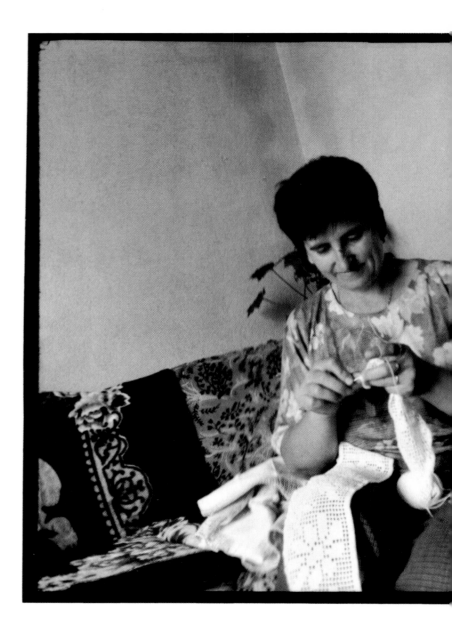

Begzada, 40, at far left, who lost her husband in the Srebrenica massacre, supports her mother and children with handicrafts.

IN WOMEN'S HANDS

*Hajrija (left) collects wild herbs,
which she dries and prepares at home before selling
them to a middleman, who distributes them
to companies that make homeopathic
medicines. Neighbors call her house the "home for
healing." Igbala (opposite) supports her
husband and two children by working as a tailor.
Her husband is ill, so she is the sole
breadwinner of her family.*

SEWING LESSON

Azra (left), a psychology student, whose father hid her and her siblings in a basement during the war, learns sewing at the women's center. Helping her is Jasmina, director of sewing, standing behind her, and Ajsa, manager of South Region for Microcredit Program, Women for Women International. Traditional crafts such as the weaving of kilim rugs (opposite) are also taught there. "I learned that as a woman who wore a scarf on her head, I can do anything I want to, and that there are no obstacles in front of me, if only I try hard enough," Azra says.

Women are safely tending fields again in Bosnia.

AT TIMES WE WERE NOT CERTAIN
WHEN IT WAS DAY AND WHEN IT WAS NIGHT,
BUT IN THE END OUR HARD WORK
PAID OFF. WE MADE SOME PROFIT
AND BOUGHT A VEHICLE.
AT FIRST, WE USED IT TO TRANSPORT
VEGETABLES AND MILK PRODUCTS TO THE
MARKET. THEN WE TURNED
OUR VEHICLE INTO A MOBILE MARKET
AND DROVE IT FROM ONE STREET
TO ANOTHER. SOON WE HAD PERMANENT
CUSTOMERS AND BUSINESS
WAS GROWING.

—ENVERA
from Orasac

WE COLLECT SCRAP METAL

LYING ALONG THE ROAD, OLD STRUCTURES

DESTROYED IN THE WAR, AND WASTE

THAT PEOPLE THROW OUT ON THE STREET.

I PICK UP METAL ALL DAY LONG.

I POUND CANS WITH A HAMMER...BUT

I AM NOT ASHAMED. I MANAGE TO MAKE

A HOT LUNCH FOR MY CHILDREN

AND PROVIDE A CLEAN AND TIDY HOME.

—SENIJA
from Gorazde

Senija, who recycles metal from war debris to earn a living.

ZEJNEBA

War has taught Zejneba (shown on the following pages) many lessons. A small one is that her name means more than "bashful person," which is what she was taught as a child.

Zejneba, 42, was born in the village of Bratunac, near Srebrenica. She married a man from Bratunac and gave birth to two children. They had cows, some land, and a life that allowed her to fall asleep thanking God for everything she had been given. Then one night, whole families—fathers, sons, husbands, and brothers—disappeared. Women were expelled from their homes. Some people were taken prisoner or killed in bloody chaos. Her husband's mother was murdered in front of their eyes.

"I can't even remember all the days clearly enough, because days and nights were mixed up for me, and they were all full of horror, chaos, fear, and uncertainty whether we would survive at all," she recalls. "We were hungry, sad, and miserable. They kept us like prisoners in our own homes."

When men heard they were going to be taken away to a camp, most likely to be killed, she and her husband took their children and ran into the forest. They met others like them among the thickets and trees, also running and running. When the children could no longer walk, they carried them through the mountainous enemy terrain. "Just keep on going, don't look back, don't be afraid, be strong, just a little farther, and you'll reach free territory," she told herself.

Finally they reached a suburb of Sarajevo and settled into an abandoned house, where they stayed until the end of the war. There were no jobs, no food. It felt hopeless. She told herself, "Be brave, you bashful person, you…think of your children, fight for them…do not be scared…there must be a way out."

With the help of microcredit loans, she bought first a cow, then land near the village of Drozgometva, and ultimately established a dairy-products business that employs her entire family.

"When I finish all of my work late at night I thank God for giving me an opportunity to survive the horror and for helping me find women who gave me self-confidence," she says. "I have grown into other meanings of myself. I have learned my name also means a tree with deep roots that keeps blooming and smells nicely for the family it shelters."

"BE BRAVE!"

*Zejneba and her husband took their children
and fled into the woods near Srebrenica to survive.
"Be brave," she told herself. Since the end
of the war, with the help of nine microcredit loans,
Zejneba has established a successful
dairy business near the village of Drozgometva.*

Želim da vani kažem ponesto i o mojoj s

Bosna je vječna

Život je vječan ali je vječna i Bosna. Prolaze vijekovi, protiču i umiču carstva i vladari a Bosna živi. Sve se mijenja a ona ostaje kakva jest. neprohodna, dobrodušna i junačka. Kroz nju vode uski putevi. Bosna je vječna a i mi u vječ smo vječni.

Želim vam puno. sreće jer je ona svakome potrebna. Puno pozdrava od mene i moje porodice.

Budite dobro   Nebić Armela

Do vašeg odgovora!

ĬRNELA   AMEL

I WANT TO TELL YOU ALSO

SOMETHING ABOUT MY BOSNIA.

BOSNIA IS ETERNAL.

LIFE IS ETERNAL, BUT BOSNIA IS ETERNAL ALSO.

THE CENTURIES ARE PASSING, THE KINGDOMS AND KINGS ARE FALLING

FROM THEIR THRONES, BUT BOSNIA LIVES FOREVER.

EVERYTHING IS CHANGING, BUT SHE STAYS AS SHE IS:

IMPENETRABLE, KIND-HEARTED, AND BRAVE.

THE ROADS ARE NARROW IN MY BOSNIA.

BOSNIA IS ETERNAL, AND WE WHO LIVE HERE, WE ARE ETERNAL TOO.

I WISH YOU ALL THE LUCK, AS EVERYONE NEEDS HER.

BEST REGARDS FROM ME AND MY FAMILY.

STAY WELL!

UNTIL YOUR LETTER....

—ANONYMOUS

A letter from a Bosnian woman, signed with the hands of her children.

THE BUSINESS OF SURVIVAL

Strong and determined,
Bosnian women come together weekly
to take part in microfinance programs that help
them rebuild their families' lives.
"Nothing is too difficult for us," says Lucija,
second from left. We are women, and women
can do anything they think of."

MOSTAR BRIDGE

*Built by a Turkish architect in 1566,
the "Old Bridge" had served as
a crossroad between East and West until
it crashed into the Neretva River in
1993 under heavy shelling by
Croatian forces determined
to separate Christian and Muslim
Mostar. The bridge was rebuilt with
international assistance and
rededicated in 2004. In a still divided
city, it stands as a symbol that peace
is often built a stone at a time.*

DEMOCRATIC REPUBLIC OF THE CONGO

WHERE THERE ARE SOLDIERS AND ARMED PEOPLE,

THERE IS RAPE. THEY USED TO HIDE AFTER THEY RAPED.

THEN, THEY STOPPED HIDING.

—IMMACULEE

Photographs by Sylvia Plachy

THE FORGOTTEN LAND

At moments, the sheer beauty of the Democratic Republic of the Congo (DRC) makes it possible to forget the magnitude of tragedy that occurred here. From 1996 to 2002, killing, rape, and preventable disease left millions of people dead and virtually every survivor scarred. Congo is a land of dazzling colors and vibrant music, of misted volcanoes and lakes so still you can sometimes hear the fall of a fisherman's net. Its storied rain forest, the second largest in the world, gives shelter to an array of rare species. Seemingly unlimited resources—timber, gold, copper, and wild rubber—have enriched kings and industrialists. Yet Congo is one of the poorest countries in the world, a nation of more than 250 ethnic groups speaking 700 languages. Located in the heart of Africa, Congo's fortunes are inextricably tied to those of its neighbors: Sudan, Uganda, Rwanda, Burundi, Tanzania, Zambia, Angola, Republic of Congo, and Central African Republic.

In the 1880s, King Leopold II of Belgium spearheaded the scramble for European control of Africa in brutal private pursuit of wealth, ruling the nation as a personal fiefdom for 23 years. Forests were stripped and villages leveled to make room for rubber plantations. Between 5 and 15 million Congolese died from disease, malnutrition, and forced labor; some workers who opposed the king had their hands cut off. Confronted with evidence of the brutality of Leopold's regime, the nation of Belgium assumed control of the colony in 1908, naming it the Belgian Congo. The worst abuses subsided. The economy grew, but Belgians kept for themselves most positions of status and influence. Though women were traditionally subordinate to men, they had played important roles in the social and political systems of some of Congo's early kingdoms; three provinces once had women rulers, and many villages observed matrilineal bloodlines. The colonial administration undermined these and other traditional social structures, often reducing women's political and economic status, as well as their access to land and household resources.

In 1960, fueled by independence movements, the Congolese wrested their freedom from Belgium. Patrice Lumumba became prime minister; but soon a power struggle ensued between Lumumba and opposition

Previous pages: A bullet-pockmarked mural at a Bukavu beauty salon.

groups, against a backdrop of the Cold War. Lumumba was assassinated with the support of the United States and Belgium. Both countries feared he was courting Soviet influence and might restrict Western access to Congo's riches. In 1965, former military leader Mobuto Sese Seko seized power and renamed the country Zaire. He ruled for 32 years, enriching himself as living standards plummeted. In the name of restoring order to a restive people, security forces conducted mass executions. The economy and state institutions, including schools and hospitals, collapsed. Preventable diseases like the deadly ebola virus and tuberculosis proliferated.

In 1994, after months of violence and genocide in neighboring Rwanda, more than a million refugees flooded across the border to Congo, including thousands of Hutu militia who had perpetrated the Rwandan genocide. A complex web of conflict, referred to as the First Congo War, ensued in late 1996. Two years later, Africa's "first world war" began, a conflict that lasted four years, involved nine African nations, and included the Hutu *Interahamwe*, a cluster of seven local militia factions created in response to Rwanda's

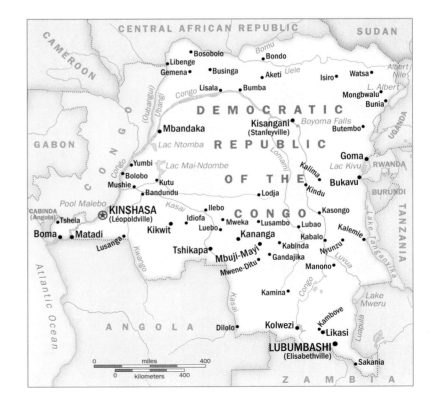

occupation of eastern Congo. Combatants also plundered Congo's modern wealth—diamonds, gold, oil, and columbite-tantalite, or coltan for short, a metallic ore refined for use in cell phones, pagers, and laptops. Refugees cut down trees to build shelter and killed endangered species for food.

Modern Africa has known no deadlier war. One study estimates that at least 3.3 million people died between August 1998 and November 2002, mostly from disease and malnutrition—the highest civilian death toll since World War II. A peace agreement signed in 2002 failed to stop terrorization of civilians and rape. A transitional power-sharing government took control with a mandate to hold elections in 2006.

During the conflict, virtually all armies systematically used rape and sexual torture to tear apart families, destroy communities, and secure their hold on territories. Combatants fortified by drugs, alcohol, and imported weapons raided towns, stealing, burning, torturing, killing, and kidnapping. With no threat of punishment, they publicly humiliated groups of women. Documented rape victims included babies as young as four months and women as old as 84 years. One

ten-year-old girl soldier forced into a militia was raped nightly by boy soldiers who believed that rape would help them move up faster in the military command. Particularly brutalized were women of the Batwa, or pygmy people, who became targets because of superstitions that having sexual intercourse with Batwa women would protect men from bullets and cure HIV.

Today, countless survivors bear visible psychological scars of rape, torture, and mutilation. Millions more carry profound psychological wounds caused by trauma and humiliation, as well as untreated HIV/AIDS. A hallmark of this conflict are countless stories of mothers and daughters who were raped simultaneously, hearing each other's screams as young girls were rendered pregnant orphans. Many victims suffer from painful, rape-induced fistulas caused by the tearing of the walls between the vagina, bladder, and anus, causing odor and a lack of bladder control that leaves them outcasts.

Rejection by husbands—and sometimes by their communities—has been one of the most difficult problems for women to bear. Under prewar Congolese law, rape was considered a crime of honor against the husband, and some husbands fled in shame over their inability to protect their women. Many women have been held responsible for their rape. Ostracized from their communities, they start their lives over in unfamiliar places, sometimes giving birth to babies who are cast out themselves because they bear the faces of attacking ethnic groups.

Amid such suffering, women in some areas are emptying their hearts of their ordeals and seeking new solutions. With the support of international organizations, local women's groups have started mediation programs and public awareness campaigns urging communities to embrace rather than shun rape survivors. Elderly women are performing traditional rites to "purify" rape victims to help family members accept them. Some fistula victims are pooling their funds to help one another undergo reparative surgery. "Listening centers" allow women to meet others who have endured similar traumas.

In one historic event in 2003, a group of women stripped naked on a public stage, bravely revealing their scarred bodies, and shouted, "If you are going to rape us, rape us now, because this must stop today!"

A year later, at an International Women's Day ceremony in Kinshasa, one of Congo's four vice presidents, a former rebel leader, publicly asked for forgiveness of the women. Many of the 3,000 women in attendance booed; his words seemed empty. Rape had not stopped simply because wartime commanders had formed a transitional government. Less than 0.1 percent of the national health program was allocated to victims of sexual violence. "Don't rape women—women are your mothers!" urges one radio campaign.

Social inequities remain. The Congo family code requires wives to obey their husbands, even if they are the primary supporters of their families. Because education is not free, families living on the equivalent of 20 U.S. cents a day often choose to send only sons to school. Women's organizations are fanning out into the countryside to educate women—and occasionally their husbands—about women's rights. Demanding a greater role in navigating the transition from war to peace, women parliamentarians have united behind a simple slogan: "Parliament, the bedrock of democracy; women, the pillar of the nation."

Si vous voulez en savoir plus, je suis à votre entière disposition.

Ma mémoire fait marche arrière et s'arrête à l'époque où jouissant d'une belle vie comme femme professionnelle et animatrice des projets de développement pour le progrès j'avais amassé fortune et planifié ma vie et celle de toute ma famille quand hélas! sont survenues survenues dans mon cher pays Congo des différentes guerres et leurs conséquences qui sont venues tous engloutir anéantir me faisant captive, esclave des tortures

viols et violences sexuels pendant plus d'une année dans les forêts loin des membres de la famille parmi des étrangers armés jusqu'aux dents qui ne s'exprimaient qu'en Kinyarwanda la langue de leur pays. Quelle horreur, répugnance, quelle vie de résignation d'impuissance, d'humiliation du ridicule pour une maman digne de son nom trop de nostalgie et de soucis. Quelle révolte! Perdant le sens de la vraie et belle vie, celle que je menais m'était insupportable, elle m'avait plongé dans la pauvreté la plus misérable portant un seul pagne déchiré et un petit tricot qui n'était même pas à ma taille.

Tirant profit d'une attaque d'un autre groupe armé je me décide de rompre avec cette vie. Pour la paix, la liberté sans soucis du pain je m'abandonne à la divine providence.

MY MEMORY GOES BACK IN TIME AND STOPS

AT A PERIOD WHEN I ENJOYED HAVING A BEAUTIFUL LIFE.

AS A PROFESSIONAL WOMAN I WAS A MANAGER OF DEVELOPMENT PROJECTS.

I WAS ABLE TO PROVIDE A COMFORTABLE LIFESTYLE FOR MY FAMILY,

WHEN, ALAS, FOR MY DEAR COUNTRY, CONGO, VARIOUS WARS BEGAN

WITH THE CONSEQUENCE OF SWALLOWING AND ANNIHILATING EVERYTHING,

MAKING ME CAPTIVE, A TORTURED SLAVE, SEXUALLY VIOLATED

FOR MORE THAN A YEAR IN THE FORESTS, FAR FROM MEMBERS OF MY FAMILY,

AMONG STRANGERS ARMED TO THE TEETH WHO ONLY SPOKE

THEIR OWN LANGUAGE, KINYARWANDA. WHAT HORRORS, REPUGNANCE,

WHAT A LIFE OF RESIGNATION, POWERLESSNESS, HUMILIATION,

AND RIDICULE FOR A MOTHER WORTHY OF THAT NAME...

—HONORATA
from Bukavu

A letter written by Honorata, former director of a technical institute for girls.

THE TIME I SPENT CAPTIVE

HAS MADE ME LOSE

ALL TASTE FOR MEN. I DO

NOT THINK MARRIAGE

IS IN MY FUTURE.

—ESPERANCE

Esperance and her son Daniel.

A wall in a family home. The writing, in French, is a child's homework.

ESPERANCE

Esperance was walking to market with her mother just after dawn one day in 2003 when two armed soldiers appeared and forced them into a stand of brush off the road. There, in an unremarkable setting they passed almost daily, they found a group of 50 others encircled by more armed militia members.

One of the soldiers went over to her. "Look at me," he told her.

"I refused to look at him," she says. "He started beating me. I started crying. He said to me, 'Why are you are crying? I can kill you. And, you would not be the first for me to kill.'"

He took his bandana and wrapped it around her head, staking his claim to her, and left to join the others. Esperance, 17, removed the bandana, but when the soldier came back, he recognized her anyway. He ordered her to carry his heavy equipment, and they set off down the road. Her mother, left behind, could only watch.

They walked for hours. Esperance tried to run off, but the soldier caught her again. Finally, some six miles farther, they reached a military encampment in the forest, where he escorted her to his small hut and raped her. The next morning, she found that 19 other young women had also been taken there. They were assembled at dawn, as if in a class, and were instructed in the ways their lives would change. Every day, they would be awakened at six in the morning to wash, cook, and clean for their captors.

"We worked hard," she recalls. "It was to your advantage to work. If you were working, you got some rest. If you were not working, you were being raped."

Several months later, pregnant and critically ill, she was sent away to die by the soldiers. Some villagers found her and took her to Panzi Hospital in Bukavu, where she received proper medical care. Somewhat restored, she gave birth to a baby boy and named him Daniel. Like many rape victims, she loves the child she knows is an innocent victim. Yet his face is a constant reminder of the soldier who enslaved her. With facial features different from her own background, Daniel, like many children born to raped mothers during this war, is treated as an outcast by many in her community.

Esperance has become the youngest member of a women's group that studies subjects that matter to them, ranging from reproductive health and entrepreneurial skills to simply sharing painful experiences with other women. She says she has found most compelling the classes about nutrition and the group's discussions about protesting war. "Why should women leave responsibility for war and peace to men," she came to wonder. "How could women afford to remain silent when it was men who fought the wars and women who suffer their atrocities?"

Esperance whose name means "hope," lives again with her mother and the child. Her life has taken on a more normal routine. The wife of the pastor of her church offered to pay for her education, enabling her to return to school. "I want to focus my energy on my studies and nothing else," she says. "My aspiration is to become a nurse."

THE TRAUMA THEY
TALK ABOUT IS THE TRAUMA
OF RUNNING FROM THEIR
VILLAGES AFTER THEY
HAVE JUST BEEN RAPED.
THEY HOLD IN THEIR
SECRET UNTIL SOMEONE
FINDS THEM.

—PROFESSOR AND PSYCHOLOGIST
KABANGA MPARDA

Panzi Hospital in Bukavu.

Marie (right), with two of her children and (opposite) with her youngest.

MARIE

A high school graduate with a teaching certificate, Marie was working at a local primary school in rural Ngweshe at the time she met her husband. They had six children during their ten years of marriage.

Then the *Interahamwe* came, slaughtering villagers, pillaging homes, and taking her and four other women deep into the Lulaba Forest, 30 miles away. She was forced to live as a sexual slave of a militia commander. Humiliated, worried for her children, she managed to escape one day when she went for water. But upon returning home, her husband told her she had become the wife of the Interahamwe. She and their children were ejected from their home. She decided to take her family to the city, in hopes of finding safety in Bukavu. They walked for three months, eating what they could find.

"One of my children got sick and died on the way," she said. "Then, after arriving in Bukavu, I found out I was pregnant, and I was so sad and depressed that I reached the point of being suicidal. The pregnancy felt like a curse after all I had been through."

A local association of women survivors of rape helped her find medical care. "Today, I have a baby girl," she said. "I volunteer to help other women who are rape survivors because of what I have been through as a rape survivor."

BUKAVU

A road leads through the eastern commercial hub of the city, as seen through the windshield of a vehicle operated by a non-governmental organization. The red circle with the X through the rifle on the windshield denotes a vehicle that carries no arms.

I WORE A CLOTH
COVERING MY ARMS
BECAUSE I WAS
ASHAMED OF THEM.

—JEANNETTE

Jeannette with her baby.
Her hands were cut off by rapists.

JEANNETTE

Jeannette and her husband used to live on a farm, with goats, cows, and chickens. To make extra money, she sold palm oil, and he worked as a carpenter. That life, that "normal" life, ended in less time than it took to change her baby's diaper.

Rwandan militants stormed into their village with machetes, guns, and boxes of matches. Jeannette and her husband fled when the soldiers set fire to their home. As she ran, she slipped and fell with her naked baby in her arms.

"The soldiers came over to me and without asking any questions, they began hitting me on the neck and collarbone with the machetes," she says without emotion. "After they were finished raping me, while I was still on the ground, they spread out my arms. I closed my eyes, believing that they were going to hack me to death. I felt the cut of the machete and fainted."

They left her there to bleed to death. When she woke up, she found herself in a hospital instead, and when she was finally able to speak, she asked about her baby. "Your baby is in an orphanage," the doctor told her, glancing at the bandages on her arms. She looked down and realized she had no hands; the soldiers had cut them off.

"People told my husband to leave me, because I was raped," she says. "He answered that his heart would not allow him to do so. My husband has been everything to me. He helps me eat. He washes and dresses me. He does everything for me."

A sympathetic priest helped procure prostheses for her arms, but they proved to be too heavy for daily use. The priest also helped find them a house, but villagers resentful of her getting advantages, forced out her family and moved into the house themselves. Jeannette learned to beg.

When a transitional government was being set up during a fragile peace, Jeannette was escorted to Kinshasa, capital of the Democratic Republic of the Congo, for an International Women's Day Celebration. Sitting in the audience were representatives of the warring parties. Onstage, women began talking about being raped and tortured during the war. That day she realized she wasn't alone.

TO SURVIVE,

I USED TO BEG.

WITH NO HANDS

PEOPLE HAD

PITY FOR ME

BECAUSE THEY SAW

THERE WAS

NOTHING I COULD

DO TO MAKE

A LIVING.

—JEANNETTE

One woman had been shot in the vagina when she was pregnant. Another was nearly burned to death.

"One woman brought me forward onto the stage and cried, 'Here is another one,' and told me to introduce myself and say what I had experienced and witnessed," she remembers. "I told them about what had happened in my village and that we did not want that to happen anymore. I wept and so did the other women. Some women were so angry that they started taking their clothes off to show what had been done to them."

It took months before Jeannette could go home again after speaking out that day. Authorities, armed with her picture, were searching for her. One woman who participated in the event was killed.

Today Jeannette is beginning to learn new skills and is hopeful her children will grow up to live a normal life, though the older children are still in an orphanage at the SOS Children's Village.

"Even if I am given food, clothes, or a house, if this war continues I will always be vulnerable," she says. "For the future, I hope for peace in the Democratic Republic of the Congo."

Jeannette with her youngest child. Authorities began searching for her after she spoke out against her attackers.

SOS CHILDREN'S VILLAGE

Jeannette's elder son,
Mapenzi, grasps the hand of
his younger brother,
Pascal, at an orphanage in Bukavu
that is sometimes referred
to as a home for children of
"irresponsible parents."

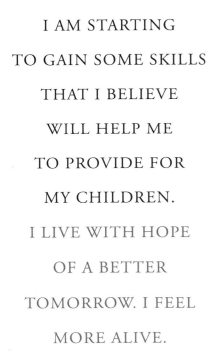

I AM STARTING
TO GAIN SOME SKILLS
THAT I BELIEVE
WILL HELP ME
TO PROVIDE FOR
MY CHILDREN.
I LIVE WITH HOPE
OF A BETTER
TOMORROW. I FEEL
MORE ALIVE.

—JEANNE
from Bushwira/Kabare

*Congolese women in a
gender-awareness session.*

82

CLAIRE

Claire wanted to be a lawyer when she was young. Even now, as a 40-year-old widow, it pains her to think about the way her dream was aborted. She was a serious student in her third year of high school and helped support her younger siblings by selling fruit. She was fetching water one day in 1984 when a young man, who wanted to marry her, abducted her with the help of friends, stuffed cotton in her mouth to stop her screams, and took her away to a house to be raped. She became pregnant.

"I did not like this man, but people from the district convinced me that I should marry him because he wanted to marry me," she says. "It is hard to go against the pressure of the community as a woman. What could I have done? I was pregnant. At that point I had to completely stop my studies, the one thing that was important to me."

She was married to him for ten years before she managed to separate and return to her village with her children. Eventually, she remarried and got a job.

Then, in 1999, the *Interahamwe* rebels attacked. "They did the most unimaginable things to me and stripped me of any sense of human dignity and self-worth," she said. They also stole everything of value she and her husband had managed to acquire and made him carry it away with them as a beast of burden. She was left behind, with their six children, injured and traumatized. Her husband later escaped, only to die of malaria.

Alone, seeking refuge from rural militia, she fled with her children to Bukavu. But as one of thousands of internally displaced persons, she could find no job. "I had nothing, and I could not find work," she said. "So I started carrying heavy, one hundred-pound loads on my back just to make a meager living. This enabled me to feed my children a few times during the week."

She was coming out of a nutrition center with her youngest daughter when she heard about a program that would allow her to go to classes to learn alternatives to her back-breaking labor and maybe one day return to school herself to become a lawyer.

"My mind is becoming more and more sharpened," she says. "I am aware of things I had never thought about."

"I used to think I was alone in having been raped and handicapped," says Jeannette, with her friend Claire, at right.

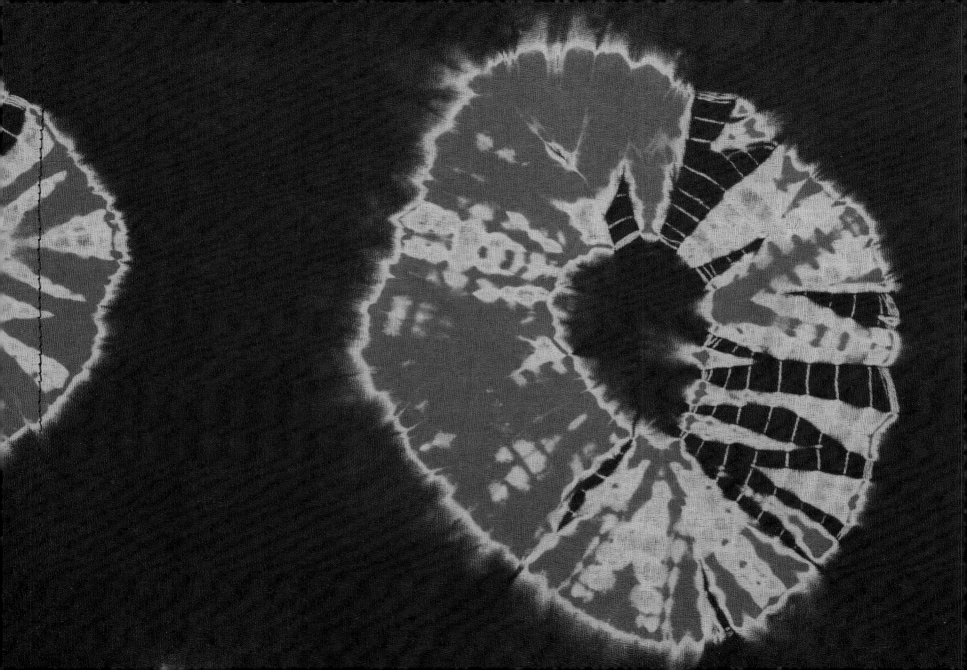

TIE-DYED FABRIC

Among the specialties in a job skills training class,

women learn to decorate fabrics by tie-dyeing.

Tying off areas that resist the dye bath,

they create patterns with strong graphic appeal and discover

how to bring a fresh twist to old techniques.

The traditional fabrics are popular in

local and regional markets.

HONORATA

Before war came, Honorata was a director of a technical institute for girls called Lycée Amani. To earn more money to help support her five children, she was also a small entrepreneur who sold basic necessities. She happened to find herself in a small mining town one day when shooting broke out between rebel armies. She and 11 other women were surrounded by soldiers.

The soldiers beat her and stretched her out on the ground. She remembers thinking that her legs and arms were stretched out in the form of a cross. One by one, the men took turns raping her—debasing her was how she thought of it. Then, the soldiers took all 12 women to a camp in the middle of a forest, where for a year the soldiers shared the women along with the chickens, food, and other booty they stole.

In the chaos of an attack on the camp by another militia, the women escaped. She and a few of the other women struck out for Bukavu. They walked for two months, sleeping outdoors in the rain or moonlight, eating almost nothing. Her only clothing was a single piece of cloth wrapped

Honorata, a former school director, tilling her field.

around her. By the time she arrived in Bukavu, her former colleagues didn't recognize her. She was finally reunited with her five children, but her husband had taken another wife. She moved in with a friend and her friend's children.

A year later, as life seemed to be returning to normal, insurgents banged on the door of their house. And Honorata, 52, began reliving the horror she thought she had escaped. This time her grown daughter, who was pregnant, was raped as well.

"Today I am healed from the bleeding," says Honorata. "But the hardest thing is the emotional pain. It is one thing to have been through what I have been through. To have gone so long without anyone acknowledging it, triples the pain. Having someone recognize my humanity again has dared me to hope."

After participating in classes on women's roles and the importance of becoming an active citizen, she stood up in front of political and community leaders on International Women's Day and called for official accountability for the suffering of Congolese women. "I did not believe that I could still hold a speech in front of a crowd," she said afterward. "But I have done just that."

A mural frames a house in eastern Congo.

I WISH FOR SCHOOLING FOR MY CHILDREN.

—A MOTHER OF TEN

I WISH FOR PEACE. WHEN WE KNOW PEACE, WE CAN BUILD OUR SOCIETY.

WITHOUT PEACE, WE CAN'T EVEN FIX OUR HOUSES.

—FURAHA

I WANT CLEAN WATER.

—VANANCEE

I ASK FOR THE INTERNATIONAL COMMUNITY TO STOP THE

FLOW OF THESE ARMS TO STOP THIS WAR.

—MIRIMBA

I WISH FOR AN AUTOMATIC POUNDER. I AM TOO TIRED TO POUND EVERYTHING

WITH MY OWN HANDS NOW.

—A WOMAN FROM NYATEMDE, NYENGO VILLAGE

ENTREPRENEURS

Congolese women traditionally perform 80 percent of the nation's agricultural labor.

During the war, however, women were prevented from growing food for fear

of attack by roving militia, and severe malnutrition spread through eastern regions once known as the

country's breadbasket. Now, women are returning to work in the fields and marketplaces,

rebuilding the economy literally from the ground up.

The voices of marketplace entrepreneurs are strong. While Cecile (right) sells mangoes to help

send her daughter to school, another woman shouts out the virtues of her hand-dyed cloth to shoppers

who tease each other as they kneel to examine her goods.

In this country, known as one of the great capitals of African music,

rumba beats pour from doorways in late afternoons.

BURDENS

Women traumatized by war, injury, and loss often wind up shouldering the heaviest burdens in post-conflict zones. As the sole support of their families, they will take on any job, many carrying heavy loads of charcoal or firewood or stones to sustain and rebuild their communities.

HAULING ROCKS

Decades of war and tyranny destroyed much of Congo's infrastructure —schools, hospitals, and roads. Cash is scarce, and there are few jobs. Women traumatized by war shoulder much of the backbreaking burden of building—rebuilding—their lives and their country. Carrying out basic acts of sustenance, they go about their daily life, gathering firewood and water, often risking attack from roving militia or rapists.

Unable to find other ways to feed their families, many carry charcoal, fruit, stones, and building materials for construction companies. Throughout ravaged areas, women hammer boulders into rocks, hoist the rocks onto their backs, and lug them to construction sites. For this work, they are paid about five U.S. dollars a month, a sum insufficient to buy one meal a day for a family of seven. Bahatee, a woman who carries stones with her daughter, says: "I don't have enough to eat. I wouldn't be carrying stones if I could have something to eat. I eat once a day. We are only able to eat one meal at night. Nothing the whole day."

Sometimes whole families carry stones. One young girl—she does not know how old she is, but her mother guesses about 14—eats nothing during the day and only a small meal at night. "My work is to carry stones," she says. "I get paid when I finish carrying the whole thing. It takes me about one month." Her youngest sister carries stones, but is not paid. "My back hurts and my stomach aches," says Cerrine. "I suffer a lot, but I don't have a choice." In markets, street children offer to carry parcels in exchange for food.

Some of those who carry stones do not have shoes.

Women who continue to haul heavy burdens, while pregnant, sometimes go into labor as they march along the road. Some women must leave their babies a few days after delivery to return to the work of hauling, exacerbating not only their own health problems, but creating nutrition deficits for the newborns, who are fed grilled banana instead of mother's milk. It is not uncommon for a woman who has carried out this work over long periods of time to have her uterus fall out of her abdomen.

The good news is that roads that were eerily empty during the conflict are lined again with women carrying pineapples, mangoes, and other goods to sell in the markets. In a few areas, with the help of nonprofit organizations, women are beginning to organize cooperatives to develop microcredit, literacy, and gender-training programs that offer less painful ways of sustaining families. One association has members who import and sell used shoes. Another purchases donkeys that members use to help them carry loads and that are rented out to other women as well. From the funds they receive through these rentals and other cooperative approaches, such as cassava-grinding machines, women are able to pay for their electricity and other costs.

Such groups also offer training in women's rights, business management, and job-training. While most members are women, a few men have also been brought into the group. "We feel good about being members of the association," says one male member. "Before, we saw women as weak, but now we see that women are organized and strong. Now I know that women are equal to me. They are human beings."

WHEN WE TALKED ABOUT GENDER, WE FELT THAT MEN SHOULD BE PART OF THE ASSOCIATION BECAUSE WOMEN AND MEN COMPLETE EACH OTHER.

—LEOCADIE

UNCERTAIN FUTURE

Passengers await a ferry that will transport them across Lake Kivu, which borders Rwanda. The area is a gateway to wildlife sanctuaries, home to famed lowland gorillas and other endangered species. During the war, even the land was violated—by plundering militias, illegal mining and logging operations, and millions of people seeking food and shelter while trying to escape genocide. This former war zone is enjoying a tenuous peace.

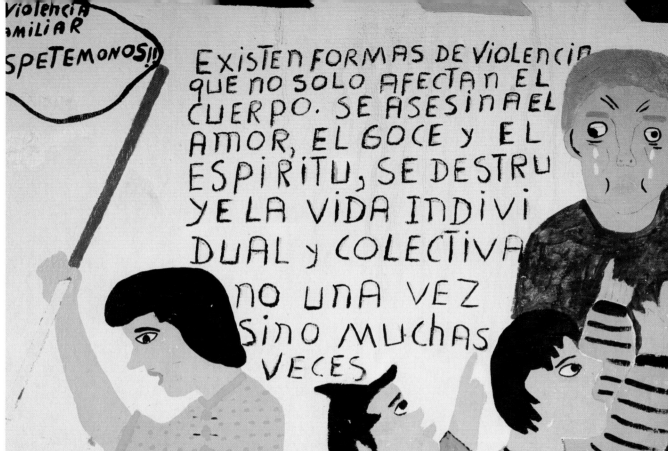

COLOMBIA

THERE EXIST FORMS OF VIOLENCE

THAT AFFECT NOT JUST THE BODY. THEY ASSASSINATE LOVE,

ENJOYMENT, AND THE SPIRIT. THEY DESTROY

INDIVIDUAL AND COLLECTIVE LIFE, NOT JUST ONE TIME,

BUT MANY TIMES.

—MURAL IN CHIQUINIMA, TOLIMA DEPARTMENT

Photographs by Susan Meiselas

THE FERMENTING WAR

It is easy to make the argument that there is no civil war in Colombia, especially in the capital of Bogotá. Except for heightened security measures, war is almost unseen in the modern metropolis, which closes its downtown for cyclists and baby strollers on Sundays and wins global prizes for urban planning.

The indisputable proof that war is real is the fact that Colombia has the largest number of internally displaced persons of any nation on earth, except Congo and Sudan. About three million citizens, most from rural areas, have been forced out of their homes since 1985 alone. Edged off the front pages by bombs and brutal genocide in the Eastern Hemisphere, Colombia's war is now in its fourth decade, despite efforts by popular President Alvaro Uribe to contain it. On an average day, 20 people may die, many assassinated in small towns and settlements. An increasing number are women.

Colombians sometimes refer to this war, one of the world's most stubborn and inbred, as a *sancocho:* a rich national dish typically made of meats, potatoes, yucca, and a variety of spices. The list of ingredients

Previous pages: Scene depicting child abuse in a mural done by the women of Chiquinima.

is long: a stunning topography of nearly inaccessible mountain valleys, a 20th-century political system that eliminated opponents through massacres and electoral exclusion, entrenched guerrillas and institutionalized paramilitary networks, a foreign-financed army, the world's premier cocaine cartel, and an indisputable predisposition to resolving personal disputes by violence. It is a war by murder and threats whose silver lining—if such a thing is possible—is a growing awareness of women to the possibility of bettering their lives and preventing physical and sexual abuse.

Colombia is an astonishingly rich and beautiful nation. With coasts on both the Atlantic and the Pacific, it is a land of snow-topped Andean peaks, vast plains, grassy prairies, dense jungles, and Amazonian rain forests. It boasts the largest number of plant and animal species per unit area in the world. Orchids hang languidly from trees in city squares. Mineral and agricultural riches abound; Colombia is a leading exporter of coffee and palm oil and is one of the top ten oil-producing countries.

Yet there are large tracts of countryside that its own citizens never see for fear of violence or lack of bus fare. Colombia has one of the world's most unequal distributions of wealth. The nation has been governed largely by civilians, but elite groups tracing their status back to colonial days have dominated the nation's land, minerals, business, banking, government, the media, and social mores. About two-thirds of its population lives in poverty, fearful of being attacked by guerrillas or paramilitaries or both.

Armed conflict in Colombia goes back to long before leftist guerrillas emerged as a force in the 1960s in the wake of the Cuban Revolution. Spanish conquistadors, administrators, and Roman Catholic clergy began settling in present-day Colombia before 1500, seeking gold and Christian souls. Indigenous people were killed or died out from disease, leaving Colombia with an indigenous culture that makes up just 2 percent of today's population. A small percentage of the population is of African heritage, descendants of slaves brought by European settlers.

Colombia won its war of independence from Spain in 1819 under Simón Bolívar and Francisco de Paula Santander; Bolívar was elected as the first president of what was then known as Greater Colombia, and Santander became the vice president. Emerging from disagreements were two political parties, the Conservatives and the Liberals. Conflict

between the parties resulted in the War of a Thousand Days, from 1899 to 1902, which cost more than 70,000 lives.

Conservatives ruled until 1930, when reformists from the Liberal party came into power and instituted, sometimes with political alliances, an ambitious social agenda including agrarian reform that helped generate economic growth and industrialization. The agrarian reforms were vehemently opposed by landowners. In 1948, a populist Liberal politician was assassinated, sparking riots in Bogotá that spread to rural areas. For the next 16 years, armed groups claiming to represent each party fought in the countryside. The period, known as *La Violencia*, left 200,000 dead and as many as two million people displaced from their homes.

The two parties finally came together in 1957, as the National Front, and agreed to alternate power every four years. This truce stopped the slaughter, but excluded everyone else from participating in politics, as the party in power was given the right to appoint every official, every governor, and every mayor. Colombia became known as one of Latin America's most stable democracies, and there were numerous reforms, but the nation's many poor rural residents remained outlying victims of inadequate health, justice, and school systems.

In the 1960s, revolutionaries, proponents of the theology of liberation that favored the poor, and television began opening the eyes of the poor to other possibilities. Insurgents like the Revolutionary Armed Forces of Colombia (FARC), with Marxist roots, promoted land reform and social equality, meting out harsh "justice." In rural zones, men who beat their wives were tied to trees. Landowners were attacked and their properties turned over to peasants.

In the late 1960s and 1970s, landowners and major business owners formed paramilitary forces to protect themselves and their property from guerrilla attacks, typically with the support—sometimes open, sometimes not—of the army. Embarking on campaigns of violence and terror, paramilitaries have been responsible for killing, torturing, and "disappearing" countless human rights and community activists, teachers, peasant farmers, health workers, and political and labor leaders. Colombia's rate of kidnapping on both sides combined to become the highest in the world, with an estimated 3,000 people still believed to be held hostage, some for many years.

During the 1980s and 1990s, the conflict became progressively worse, entangled with arms trade and drug production and trafficking. The guerrillas have been associated with coca production in remote highlands, while paramilitaries have been associated with marijuana production at lower elevations. Many young men came to see their only alternatives as joining guerrillas or paramilitary or army forces. Some small villages have been left virtual ghost towns as women, left alone, finally picked up their families and fled to shantytowns ringing large cities, abandoning millions of hectares of small farms.

Colombia offers advanced legal protections for internally displaced persons, including transitional payments to help with housing, but many lack documents to prove their status—or are too afraid to declare the threats against them. One head of family returned recently to reclaim the house she had been forced to abandon, only to be told she had to pay interest on four years' worth of utility bills owed by paramilitaries who had occupied her house. Why, she wanted to know, had the government not cut off the lights?

A revised constitution developed in the early 1990s took huge strides toward recognizing human rights and addressing discrimination against women. But domestic abuse is endemic in some areas irrespective of war, and displaced women are at far greater risk of violence. A quarter of all displaced women report being raped. Abortion for any reason is a crime in largely Catholic Colombia; legalizing it under certain circumstances is now a matter of national debate. Failed abortions are among the leading causes of maternal mortality in the country. "Social cleansing" campaigns still threaten women and men who test social or political norms. One woman with four children had her womb split open by paramilitaries who called her "a whore" for attending meetings instead of staying at home with her children.

Women's groups generally oppose a government "peace with impunity" campaign that rewards paramilitary leaders with checks, while the families they victimized live with unfulfilled promises of access to schools and health care. Uribe stands against negotiations with guerrillas absent a ceasefire, favoring instead an aggressive military solution with strong support from the United States. Colombia receives the largest amount of U.S. foreign aid after Israel, Egypt, and Iraq. U.S. funds are now directed toward military purposes, though drug eradication is still a major goal.

Mix into this sancocho, this Colombian stew, a pervasive 21st-century consumerism and the ever present lure of quick drug money, and children become easy targets. Marginalized girls as young as 12 and 13, some already abused at home, offer sex in exchange for a meal, a cell phone, or a new blouse. The teen birthrate in Colombia, once relatively low, has begun to rise. With the social fabric ripping apart at the seams, the number of abandoned children is growing. One mother publicly petitioned her city government to take over her seven children.

Still, Colombia has strong civil organizations. National debate is vigorous. Women have established "women's peace routes," where caravans drive into conflict zones to express solidarity with local people who are building their own schools and community kitchens or meeting in small groups to learn how to take advantage of courts aimed at finding legal resolutions to rural and domestic conflicts. "The one thing that we know works is educating women about their rights," says Natasha, director of Colombians Helping Colombians in Ibagué, department of Tolima. "That changes lives."

Milena at her home in the indigenous community of Guaipa.

MILENA

Like most children, Milena learned in school about how Spaniards came to the Americas seeking gold and Christian souls. The more recent history of what happened to the lands their descendants occupied she learned at home.

A descendant of the Pijao, a warrior tribe that once cultivated crops near rivers, Milena tells the story passed down to her from her great-grandmother. Decades ago, she says, a wealthy landholder who owned a cattle ranch adjacent to their ranch was very generous to her family, which was poor. Whenever he slaughtered one of his cows, he would bring them meat. Then, one day he came instead with a document and told them to sign. The document was title to their land.

"You already owe me more for the meat than the land is worth," he said. Her great-grandmother, lacking the money to repay him, signed.

She went to court to try to get her title back and lost. That land was never recovered.

Milena is a sinewy veteran of many battles. When she was a little girl, she tired of watching a wealthier classmate constantly pick on her older sister, so she picked up a stone one day and hit her in the head. She took the beating her father gave her, but the girl never teased her sister again. Talk to her for five minutes, and you realize her brain is always considering her next move.

Milena began her own battle for land in 1985, when as a single mother she helped organize 17 indigenous families to petition the government for recognition as an indigenous organization with rights to claim land under a program that reimburses landholders for their properties. Coordinating with other indigenous groups, the families invaded a large ranch near her home and set up housekeeping. It was during that struggle that she met her husband, Julio, an outspoken organizer, and they had a son, now 14.

As often happens in such cases, the government stepped in to negotiate with landholders, who are typically absentee owners, and deeded the property to her community as an official *resguardo,* a parcel of land operated communally by a board of indigenous leaders with broad powers to establish their own laws.

Julio was treasurer of the board of governors of the resguardo. Milena sometimes helped him with the math. But the board was all male and refused to allow women to be members or hold title to property. She appeared before the board of governors and asked to become a member. The board turned her down. Julio, they said, represented her family.

Meanwhile, threats from paramilitaries escalated. Sometimes initials of the groups would be sprayed on local walls. Julio disappeared and his body was found at the bottom of a river; he had been shot in the head. She never found out who pulled the trigger. She knew only that he died in a battle for land.

Her first thought was to take her two young sons and flee. Then someone reminded her that she had publicly criticized another widow for giving up the struggle after her husband was assassinated, so she stayed, hiding in different homes when a lookout sighted paramilitaries.

Because women were not permitted to own land, the godfather of her two-year-old son tried to take away in his name the land she and Julio had farmed. "Who gave birth to my son?" she argued. "Who worked that land and protected it? I did." She won her battle, enabling women to hold title to property for the first time. In 1998, she became governor of the resguardo, which had grown by then to 35 families.

She still lives with threats. A year ago, a neighbor saw paramilitaries with rifles pointed toward her house and warned her to stay away from home for a while. "I've had several threats," she acknowledges with something like a smile. "But not this year. Not yet." In the last year alone, the mayors of two neighboring towns have been shot. A female professor suspected of being a guerrilla was shot in the town square, and no one dared to go to her assistance for fear of being seen as a leftist sympathizer. Though there has never been a single military engagement near her home, 17 women she knows have been widowed by assassinations.

A few years ago, Milena participated in training sessions to help raise women's awareness about such issues as health, business, and conflict resolution. While she ponders her next organizational goals, she focuses on a project that grew out of those sessions: a chicken cooperative that produces *huevos de criollo*—eggs laid by chemical-free, free-range chickens.

Asked what advice Milena would give to other women struggling for their rights, she says, "You start by asking for a word." Then, waving her hand in the air like an eager student in the back row who is repeatedly overlooked by the teacher, she adds, "But know what you will do if they don't call on you."

WOMEN GOSSIP BECAUSE WHEN THEY ARE KEPT IN THEIR HOMES, THEY HAVE NOTHING ELSE TO DO BUT WATCH COMINGS AND GOINGS. GOSSIP IS THE ENEMY OF WOMEN.

—MILENA
from Guaipa, Tolima

STILL WATERS

Milena draws water from the well
that brought water to her neighbors. She wants it known
that a friend named Luzmila, although not shown here,
was one of four people who dug the 32-foot-deep
well by hand. The last few feet were pure stone. The mother of
six children, Luzmila usually sits silently with her
nine-year-old daughter in her lap. Everywhere she goes,
she carries her daughter, who has cerebral
palsy, because there is no wheelchair, and she does
not want to leave her at home.

WAR ISN'T JUST ABOUT BOMBS

AND PEOPLE WOUNDED.

THAT'S NOT WAR. WAR IS WHAT

YOU LIVE EVERY DAY.

IT IS CONFLICT IN YOUR COMMUNITY.

HERE WE HAVE HAD

NO BATTLES.

BUT WE HAVE HAD MANY DEAD.

—MILENA
from Guaipa

Milena and her son on a bicycle outside their home.

THE WOMEN OF ROVIRA

It is a peaceful drive to the verdant foothills of Rovira, a quiet town of perhaps 27,000, which was once a tourist refuge from the steamy provincial capital of Ibagué. But beyond the highway lies territory contested at times by guerrillas, paramilitaries, and common thieves.

It is from towns like Rovira that many of Colombia's three million displaced persons come. Colombia has no refugee camps. Instead, displaced persons register for federal subsidies to cover food and transitional housing. But the system works slowly, and many are afraid to register or cannot document their flight.

An estimated 400 families have fled Rovira, many from small hillside settlements outside the city. Some have been threatened by guerrillas who fear they are police informants. Others are suspected to be guerrilla sympathizers because their sons or nephews are unaccounted for. Women are targeted by both sides to serve as runners in schemes to extort money from local businesses. A few years ago, the mayor was assassinated. So was the wife of a teacher.

Gone is the Sunday evening tradition of walking around the town square; people do not go out after dark. "Here, we stopped talking to strangers," says Nubia, 41, the mother of three and a key member of a women's sewing cooperative called *Roviconfecciones*. "We have lost all trust."

It is all the more remarkable, then, that a group of women came together for a series of gender-based classes taught by a nonprofit group called Colombians Helping Colombians. "No one thought about the women of Rovira," says Nubia. Not even the women themselves.

As part of gender-based training, women selected entrepreneurial projects ranging from planting trees to starting the sewing co-op, which sells its products door to door and to schools. They expanded a church program on preventing child abuse that safeguards children while their mothers work.

As the women talked to each other, they came to focus on domestic violence and sexual molestation they had experienced as children. Nubia, who had studied bank administration in college before the father of her three children took to padlocking her inside her home out of jealousy, found the strength to separate from him permanently. Today she encourages women to file legal complaints against abusive husbands in family circuit courts that are beginning to reach into rural areas. She also started two new women's groups: dance and basketball.

"Before, I volunteered at the church, but nothing more," said Luzmelida, one of the town's most active organizers. "Now I participate in the politics of the city. I have learned that we women are forgers of our own future."

Lulu, at left, and Magda Marleny learn sewing as part of a cooperative called Roviconfecciones *that designs, sews, and markets clothes to the community.*

SANCTUARY

The women of the sewing cooperative—from left to right,
Ana Ruth, Alba Luz, Nubia, Magda Marleny, Yeimy, and Lulu—
gather in Rovira's main square in front of Santa Gertrudis
Catholic Church. They were meeting in the square,
when they heard the tacatacataca *of a guerilla attack. Knowing that army*
retaliation may come from a plane, they ran into the church
and split up to pray, each in a different pew.
"The ghost plane detects heat from bodies, so it can't tell us
from the guerillas," explains Alva Luz, using the popular nickname for a
high-tech army aircraft that seems to appear out of nowhere.
"The people get caught between two sides."

Women of Rovira get together for a cookout.

Gatherings are often about learning to trust again.

ONE FAMILY'S LONG NIGHT

Three hundred yards from their farm, Angela and her family saw the bus across the road, a roadblock typically used by guerrillas to stop cars in order to net kidnap targets for ransom. It was Christmas Eve, and they were headed to their rice farm just 15 minutes outside the fast-growing state capital of Ibagué.

Her brother Guillermo was driving. A guerrilla in camouflage and rain boots signaled him to pull over. Instead, Guillermo put on the brakes and turned the wheel. There was a hail of bullets. The car careened into the ditch. Guillermo died of a single shot in the back, the third of Angela's brothers to be shot in the back by a guerrilla bullet on this highway in less than three years.

"You see, we had a sort of family pact that we would never pay a ransom," says Angela, 52, a social worker, fighting tears just weeks after the latest assassination. "We used to talk about it around the dinner table. We didn't want to pay kidnappers because with that money they would only buy more arms. I think my parents instilled strong values in us, to love the land and to respect life. My father was never in agreement with violence."

Her father Angelo had come to Colombia from Italy with his parents, seeking freedom from the hunger and violence they had known during World War I. He married a young Colombian woman named Nina, bought land, dug irrigation channels, planted rice, and established a *finca*—a farm—that would eventually include a rice-processing plant known for its modern technology.

There were eight children in the family, five sons and three daughters: an agronomist, a mechanical engineer, a veterinarian, a systems engineer, a philosopher, a psychologist, a social worker, and a crop-dusting pilot. Each member of the family contributed to the farm or the community around it. They patented new machinery, developed advanced seeds, increased productivity, and ran a rice-processing plant that employed 50 people. Together, Angela feels, they made a whole.

Her father understood poverty, she says, paid employees well, saw to it workers were educated, and had close relationships—*compadrazgo*—with many employee families. Unlike many landowners, they didn't hire paramilitaries. Nor did they carry arms or hire bodyguards. "Why would we?" Angela asks. "We never had any threats."

Perhaps because he had always thought of himself as an Italian peasant, his family had managed to avoid the sort of ingrained political violence that is sometimes handed down through generations here.

That changed at 7 a.m. on February, 26, 2002, when two of her brothers and two employees were driving into the finca and four guerrillas accosted them and took them off in a truck. Refusing to be kidnapped for ransom, they jumped out. The guerrillas opened fire. Yesid, 49, the crop duster, and Julio, 37, the mechanical engineer, were shot in the back. A nephew was injured.

Her father was in the finca when he heard about his sons. Afterward, he could not bring himself to leave. "He died of sadness," she says. The death of her third brother feels to her as if it has broken the family. Her mother is in a monastery praying and seeking peace. One of her two remaining brothers lives in Europe. The only sibling who remains at the finca is the veterinarian, who refuses to leave. "He doesn't want to let them win," she says, her eyes welling with tears.

Angela, who has worked with children and families of displaced persons, is herself displaced. She had to flee to Bogotá and does not have a job. A single mother, she worries about her traumatized daughter, who hid in a rice field that night as guerrillas went on to kill a second man, shoot a leg off a child, and injure a woman bus passenger before speeding off on motorbikes.

"My father was very sympathetic to many issues of socialism," she says. "Being a social worker, I am, too. Such ideas resonate where there is so much poverty. But what is the ideology behind killing my brothers? What I want the whole world to know, especially Europe because it still has idealized notions of the left, is that today the left in Colombia isn't about ideas. It is about capital."

Lest anyone think her judgment is partisan, she adds: "The same is true with the right. Drug money corrupted everything in Colombia. Ideas ended. Ideologies ended. And the government isn't defending the citizen. Everything is about fast money from drugs."

She feels as if her family and Colombia itself are passing through a long, dark night of biblical proportion.

"We were so united," says Angela. "Now, we're separated. None of us knows what to do. We are passing through doubt."

VILMA

"The women's workshops I went to taught me how to confront the problems in my life," says Vilma, 34, of Ortega.

Horrifically abused by an adoptive mother, she grew up knowing no norms for family life. Talking to other women about child abuse made her rethink many patterns in her own life: the constant mealtime arguments, the fights with her husband, the way she treated her own children.

"The workshops opened my eyes like a cow," she says, referring to gender-based classes run by Colombians Helping Colombians. "I am changing. I used to explode. No more. I used to hurt my children —not always, but sometimes. Now, I sit down and talk with them."

For years, she had fought with her husband. She tried talking with him instead. He worked in the fields, and their small house on the riverbank flooded with every rain. Instead of fighting with each other, she told him, they should work together to get ahead. She told him she wanted to go back to school to get her high-school diploma. Reluctantly, he agreed that she could go to night school. In the meantime she had developed lung cancer, but did not let it stop her.

In school she loved philosophy. Chemistry, she says, was so hard it almost killed her. But she got her high-school diploma and, seeing her success, her husband decided to go back to school, too. She is tutoring him in trigonometry and philosophy. He hopes to become an auto mechanic. She wants to work in an office and find an apartment away from the river.

IN A SENSE,

THIS WAR HAS SHED

A SPOTLIGHT ON

OUR PROBLEMS.

—VILMA
from Ortega

Vilma, the mother of three, was also fighting a battle with lung cancer when she returned to school to get her high-school diploma.

123

THE GRANDMOTHERS OF CHIQUINIMA

Many of Chiquinima's women are grandmothers who survived decades of violence and hard labor. Yet somehow, they have learned to giggle.

Sitting in an open-air chapel, with a crucifix made from two long fluorescent bulbs tied together, most speak of lives of constant deprivation and suffering. Virtually all were beaten as children and again as wives. Virtually all are separated or widowed. Yet, their collective sense of humor is unmistakable. In the midst of ongoing war, they have managed to outlive, outlast, outwork, and outsmart their oppressors.

Some are old enough to remember the first civil war, *La Violencia,* which took 200,000 lives when Colombia's two political parties fought each other for power half a century ago. "I had just had my baby an hour before when we had to flee into the hills," recalls Jova, 73. "My husband put a cowskin over my head to protect me and the baby from the rain."

Inez, 47, was allowed to go to school for a few weeks each spring as a small child before being pulled out to work in the coffee harvest and sugarcane fields. Her favorite class was recess, she says, because it was the only time she was allowed to play. Today she is a leader in her village.

Evangelina, 65, is blind in one eye from a beating by her husband. "I told him if he touched me again, I'd take him to court," she says, adding coyly, "my eyes are open now."

Her eye-opening began with a series of gender-based workshops in which women learned that they could stop men from beating their wife, that they had a right to education, and that despite war and their advanced age they could change their own lives. "After the workshops, I began to respect myself," says Evangelina. "I began to *feel.*"

One of the hardest lessons they learned was that they themselves were abusing their children and grandchildren left in their care as the intervening generation went to fight or find work in wartime.

At the time, women's groups were staging a peace march in parts of Colombia. The women of Chiquinima decided to do something more lasting and painted a mural on a wall right in the middle of Chiquinima. None of the women was an artist, but Alicia, 62, knew how to draw. Everyone else picked up brushes to paint.

"The mural is about violence against children, against old people, against women, against one another," Alicia says. In one frame, a pregnant woman is being beaten by her husband. In another, a man with

*Evangelina on
her way to work at the
women's fish farm.*

Untangling a fishnet.

a shopping list is spending the family food money on drink. In another, perhaps the most painful, children cry as mothers beat them.

The mural stayed and was admired in Chiquinima.

Next, the women decided to use skills they had learned in entrepreneurship classes and started a fish farm. Why a fish farm? "Because ours was broken," someone says, and they all laugh. Chiquinima's fish farm had been abandoned decades earlier as part of a forgotten government project. Three times it had failed, finally turning into a hopelessly overgrown bog.

After getting technical advice and a small loan, the grandmothers set up a work schedule and started digging with picks through a thicket of deep-rooted grasses and brush. Then they dug out decades of mud that had fallen into the pond from eroding hillsides. "Pigs," they called each other because they spent so much time stuck in mud. Finally, they built a retaining wall around the pond, took out another loan, and stocked the pond with baby *cachama*, a reddish fish popular in the region.

"The hens are trying to crow," a few village men said. "Don't they know only cocks can crow?"

Birds swooped down and snacked on baby fish. Snakes they had never seen before invaded from the jungle. Caimans, a crocodile-type reptile that had reportedly become naturalized after a veterinarian had tried to farm them for leather in a nearby valley, invaded the pond. The women picked up rifles and went hunting.

The fish the women pulled in with their nets proliferated. The pond doubled as a swimming hole. They built another pond. When they encountered drainage problems, they emptied both, let them rest as advised, and set about improving the design.

They set up a community store and opened a restaurant. Alicia, who serves as chef, accountant, and artist, came up with the recipes—cachama stewed, grilled, fried, breaded, steamed. Cachama in empanadas, in not-quite-traditional sancocho. Cachama catered for special events, cachama specials for Mother's Day with complimentary *chicha*.

Evangelina brews the chicha, a lightly fermented drink made of corn. Some cooks make it in two or three days. Her special recipe can take a week. "I like to work hard," she says.

I USED TO ACCEPT EVERYTHING AS MY FATE....

BUT, AFTER THE WORKSHOPS,

I BEGAN TO RESPECT MYSELF.

I BEGAN TO FEEL.

—EVANGELINA, AGE 74

from Chiquinima

Chiquinima's fish farm has been excavated, maintained, and operated by women.

HUSK EARS OF RED CORN AND SCRAPE KERNELS INTO WATER.

LET SIT FOR A DAY.

RINSE AND PUT INTO LARGE POTS MADE OF GUAYABA WOOD.

FERMENT. DRAIN CORN AND GRIND IT.

STEW LIKE SOUP. TAKE HALF THE MIXTURE OUT

AND LET IT RISE LIKE YEAST.

AFTER IT HAS RISEN, MIX IT WITH REMAINING CORN

AND LET SIT FOR A DAY. BRING TO A BOIL OVER A STRONG WOOD FIRE.

STIR CONSTANTLY FOR 12 HOURS.

IF YOU LIKE IT SWEET, DRINK IMMEDIATELY.

IF YOU LIKE IT STRONG,

FERMENT IT FOR THREE DAYS MORE.

—EVANGELINA
CHICHA RECIPE

Residents of Chiquinima cool off on a hot day.

AFGHANISTAN

WHEN OUR HUSBANDS WERE BEATEN BY THE TALIBAN,

THEY REALIZED FOR THE FIRST TIME IN THEIR LIVES THAT IT HURT TO BE BEATEN.

MEN WENT THROUGH A LOT DURING THE TALIBAN

AND THAT, IN MANY WAYS, MADE THEM MORE SYMPATHETIC

TO WOMEN'S SITUATION.

—RAGUL

Photographs by Lekha Singh

133

TYRANNY THROUGH THE KITCHEN DOOR

Long before world powers accused Afghanistan's ruling Taliban of supporting international terrorism, the terror the Taliban was imposing on its own people, especially its women, was an open secret. In the name of God, in the name of *honoring* women, the Taliban brutally enforced laws forbidding women to work, to laugh out loud, or even to wear shoes that made a sound.

A mountainous, sparsely populated Asian crossroads, Afghanistan has been conquered by armies going back to King Darius of Persia and Alexander the Great of Greece, producing a nation deeply scarred by invasion and occupation. Most of Afghanistan's population is Pashtun, accounting for 38 to 44 percent, followed by Tajik with 25 percent, Hazara with 10 to 19 percent, and smaller groups. The country's 20 different ethnic groups and its spectacular, forbidding topography make it difficult to govern; its wars are waged not only over territory or foreign control, but over fiercely held values involving religion, tribal loyalty, and political systems and urban/rural divisions.

Previous pages: A cemetery outside Kabul, where marginalized people have staked the graves of their dead with sticks and scraps of cloth.

The modern Afghan nation was founded in 1747 by Ahmad Shah Durrani, a Pashtun conqueror, who built an empire that reached from eastern Persia to the Indian Ocean and northern India. He established a lasting legacy of a strong central government that nonetheless allowed tribal chiefs great autonomy in ruling their own people. After fighting two wars with the British in the 19th century, Afghanistan found its modern-day borders drawn by agreements between the British and the Russians.

Throughout its turbulent history, Afghanistan's rulers have issued their policies by laws involving women. In the late 19th century, the otherwise ruthless Abdur Rahman Khan made the first attempts to reform customary laws pertaining to women, selectively adopting some progressive practices, while reinforcing Muslim traditions that assured women certain rights. After his assassination in 1919 his son, Amanullah Khan, became a national hero by winning full independence from Britain. The new Soviet Union, interested in keeping both Britain and its own restive Muslim citizens at bay in the wake of the Russian Revolution, offered the king technical and financial support.

Working within an Islamic framework, King Amanullah rapidly introduced reforms to modernize his nation, which was 95 percent illiterate and did not yet use a solar calendar. He updated clothing, trade, and weapons production and established the rudiments of public health and secular education systems. Through new civil and criminal codes and Afghanistan's first constitution he abolished slavery, banned prisoner torture, guaranteed civil rights, discouraged the forced seclusion of women, established a civil court system, and removed some matters of family law, Sharia, from the jurisdiction of mullahs.

Yet his trade policies led to a backlash against foreign exploitation, and his reforms ultimately served as little more than a future to-do list. In the end, he alienated both traditional religious leaders and his own army. Forced to abdicate in 1929, he left Afghanistan to royal family members who chose less dramatic paths.

In 1933 Mohammad Zahir Shah succeeded to the throne, and over the years his government experimented with reforms leading to greater political freedom. Women were eventually encouraged to enter fields such as medicine and education. They were given the right to vote

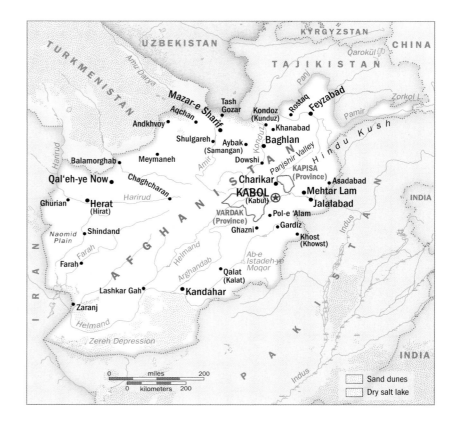

and participate in elective politics under a new constitution in 1964. Kabul became an international tourism center and was known for its cafes and theaters. An economic crisis led to a 1973 coup by former Prime Minister Daoud Khan, deposing the king. Khan's own reform attempts ultimately destabilized the country and catapulted it into the arms of the Soviet Union.

The People's Democratic Party of Afghanistan (PDPA), a communist party with links to the Soviet Union, took power through a violent coup in 1978 that killed Khan and many of his family members. The new rulers, heavily dependent on Soviet support, imposed a modernization campaign that flew in the face of Afghan tradition and Islam. Determined to replace traditional religious law with secular law, the PDPA outlawed tribal courts, forced men to cut their beards, banned women's full-length *burquas*, and forbade visits to mosques. Gender equality campaigns made education compulsory for girls and boys and abolished the concept of dowry, the tradition of giving money or property as a gift to the bride upon her marriage.

Fighting this assault on their culture, conservative "freedom fighters," later known as the *Mujadhidin*, took up arms. To quell them, the Soviet army invaded in 1979, took Kabul by force, and settled in for a bitter decade of occupation. The United States, Pakistan, and Saudi Arabia, anxious to halt Soviet expansion, helped arm and finance the Mujadhidin.

The ensuing war outlasted the Cold War and the Soviet Union itself. By the time Russian troops finally withdrew in 1989, more than a million people had been killed, six million Afghan refugees had fled to Pakistan and Iran, and two million Afghans had been displaced. Years of chaos and upheaval followed, as warlords, absent a common enemy, fought each other for power. In the process, much of Kabul was destroyed. Torture, murder, and rape seemed almost endemic.

Emerging as victors were the Taliban, or "religious students," who included fighters trained in Mujadhidin-controlled refugee camps in Pakistan, who imposed their own ruthless order on the eviscerated nation. At first, many Afghans were relieved by the Taliban efforts to reduce lawlessness and violence. But the Taliban instigated one of the most repressive regimes in modern history. In the name of upholding the tenets of Islam, the fundamentalist Taliban issued onerous laws against women that far exceeded the rules of traditional Islam. Women and girls were forbidden to attend school, work, play sports, or appear in public without a male relative. Outdoors, women were required to wear burquas that covered their bodies from head to toe. Television, makeup, nonreligious music, the Internet, and kite-flying (a national pastime) were banned. Women were forbidden to see male doctors, and female health declined.

Some women were virtually locked in their homes for years at a time. In some villages, their windows were painted so as to not allow them to see out. The Department for the Promotion of Virtue and Prevention of Vice monitored women's and men's behavior and meted out often extreme and violent punishment, including death. Beatings and executions regularly took place in soccer stadiums. During this time, some women risked imprisonment, torture, or death to work clandestinely and organize underground schools for girls with smuggled books. Women writers in the western city of Herat discussed banned foreign literature at a sewing school, hiding notebooks under their fabric.

In 2001, the people of Afghanistan were once again buffeted by global events after the terrorist organization al-Qaeda attacked New York's World Trade Center and Washington's Pentagon on September 11, 2001, killing almost 3,000 people. The U.S. government accused the Taliban of allowing terrorist groups to train on Afghan soil and of harboring al-Qaeda's Saudi militant Osama bin Laden. In October 2001, the United States funded a group of anti-Taliban warlords known as the Northern Alliance—an ethnically mixed group of former Mujadhidin—and invaded.

The Taliban fell, and the United Nations brokered an agreement establishing the Afghan Transitional Administration (ATA) headed by Hamid Karzai. The ATA ratified a new constitution, Karzai was elected president, and a new parliament was elected in September 2005. The new government has taken historic steps to represent the interests of its diverse ethnic groups and honor the country's strong Muslim heritage, but with mixed results. Much of the country remains under the control of former warlords. In the aftermath of war, the country remains littered with land mines.

Women have shouldered a tremendous burden during the long years of Afghanistan's conflicts. Thousands have been widowed and must provide for their families in a shattered economy. Many who were forced to flee the country are returning to face hardship, hunger,

and disease. Severe psychological trauma from years of violence and abuse is common. One in sixteen Afghan women dies while giving birth—more than almost anywhere in the world.

Resurgence of an organized Taliban and similar groups in some areas poses great risk to women's security and restricts their mobility. Some farmers, unable to repay drug traffickers for seeds, are returning to the traditional practice of handing over sisters and daughters as payment to creditors. Forced marriage and domestic violence are still widespread. Some women see suicide as the only way out: 75 were reported to have immolated themselves in 2005 in Herat alone.

Educated women are resuming public roles in government, nonprofit organizations, and media. Behind battered walls, women intersperse talk of current hardship with talk of a future. "My first priority when I go to Parliament will be peace, security, and stability—and to collect all the guns from warlords," said Malalai Joya, one of 68 women elected to the lower house of parliament. The number of women in parliament is slightly above the 25 percent minimum guaranteed under the new constitution.

Only about 15 percent of Afghan women are literate, but thousands of rural women are now attending literacy classes. Nearly 35 percent of the five million children enrolled in 2005 were girls, some of them 10-year-olds going to school for the first time. When Kabul University— once one of Asia's finest—re-opened in 2002 after a four-year shutdown, officials had to extend the deadline; so many young women showed up, there wasn't time for them all to take entrance exams.

Nadia tries to cover the left side of her face, scarred by a rocket explosion.

NADIA

Nadia was just a girl when she realized she had to become a man. For her first nine years, she lived as normal a life as it was possible in Kabul, a city that barely remembered peace. Her father earned a meager salary at the government's ministry of health. Her mother tended to her family and a home she remembers as wrapped around a small and beautiful garden. (Behind Kabul's warren of dust-colored walls live passionate gardeners who cultivate jasmine and roses.)

In 1996, a rocket came out of nowhere and landed on their house. She isn't sure who fired the rocket or why. But in the fire that followed, their home was destroyed, her eldest brother, 20, was killed, and Nadia suffered such severe injuries that she remained in the hospital for two years. When she was released, she was an 11-year-old girl with one ear, one eyebrow, and hair on only one side of her scalp. The left side of her head was disfigured. Her complexion was scarred from burns.

The scars left on her family were worse. Her father had been the principal breadwinner of the family. As he was reliving the nightmare of watching his eldest son die, he seemed to lose both his mind and his job. Her mother had developed a serious heart condition and was reliant on medicine she couldn't pick up because women were not permitted to leave their home, even to work, without a male. Her two younger sisters had little food and clothing and no hope of being educated. "I realized that I had to do something about it or my family would go hungry," Nadia says. "I decided that my best choice was to put my brother's clothes on and work as a boy. I remember the day I told my father I needed to do that. He had both a look of discomfort and surrender in his eyes. He, too, realized that we didn't have that many options, so he agreed."

The first job she found was as a construction laborer, making and carrying bricks. She avoided talking to coworkers and ate lunch all alone because she didn't know how to interact with them safely. Then, one day, a coworker invited her to join them. "These boys and men became my friends," she says. "Over the years, I learned their stories and their pains. They were poor just like me, and each one of them had his own story."

She took on whatever jobs she could find—herding cows, digging wells, and selling vegetables at the market for farmers. As she matured, it became harder to hide her identity. When she got her period, she was scared she would be discovered, but she found ways to disguise her needs. She learned to embrace her deformities because they assured her work and mobility. When people looked at her, especially from the left, they didn't see a boy or a girl, they saw a victim of war.

She was nearly found out one day. When she was leading a donkey carrying potatoes across the street, a car filled with Taliban members screeched to a halt to avoid hitting her. The men were furious that they had to slam on their brakes, and they got out and started beating her hard with sticks.

"I couldn't do anything," she says. "I just tried to scrunch up into a ball so I could protect my body from their sticks. By the time they were done, I was bleeding, and I could barely walk from the pain. I forced myself to get up, take the donkey, and walk back to the owner."

The donkey's owner, angry at first because she was late returning from the market with money from selling his potatoes, wanted to remove her clothing to clean the wounds on her chest. Politely, firmly, she managed to extricate herself and fled back to the room where her family was living. The wounds were so deep they needed stitches, but she could not risk going to the hospital.

Constantly in fear of discovery, she moved her family from one single room to the next. She wanted to learn to read and write, but couldn't go to school because she was afraid of being found out. When the Taliban were expelled, and a girls' school opened, she decided to confide in the principal. "I explained to her my secret and asked her to let me go to her school," she says.

So, at age 14, she pulled a woman's chador over her men's clothing and started yet another life. Other girls sat as far from her as possible,

because she smelled of sweat and garbage from the work she did after school. She pulled her scarf down over the left side of her face, but she was still teased because of her scars.

She proved to be such a quick learner that a sympathetic classmate offered her a place to live in exchange for tutoring her younger brother. Nadia heard about a sponsorship program through Women for Women International that offered classes and a monthly stipend to help support her family. At first, she attended the classes just for the stipend, feeling as isolated as she had when she first began working with men. Then, she began listening as women talked about common concerns ranging from their lack of economic opportunities to domestic violence. "I was silent in most of the classes," she said. "My mind was focused on surviving for so long that I never thought about these issues."

In the course of class discussions, she experienced a sudden awakening: her plight wasn't immutable. She could go to college. She could fight to achieve these women's rights—these human beings' rights—she never knew existed. She began to cry. She couldn't stop.

"It was the first time I felt as a woman," she says. "And other women were around me, comforting me as I cried and cried and cried."

Quickly, she mastered her job-training skills and got a position training women to cut the semiprecious stones that are used to make Afghanistan's trademark jewelry. The day she started was the first time she had worked openly as a woman. "I will never forget how it felt to

be clean, and how no one escaped from me when I got close to them," she says. "I smelled good. I had on clean women's clothes, and it felt good not to have others repelled by my smell."

A year and a half later, when she had saved enough money to go to school, she quit her job to study for university entrance exams so she could become a lawyer.

Today, at the age of 19, when many other young women are already married, Nadia lives a life she cobbled together as a child to allow her and her family to survive—at times as a woman, at times as the man who is their sole support. Willing to tell her story to the world, she remains nonetheless disguised at home. Few people know her name.

She cannot imagine marrying. "Never!" she says in the English she has learned in school. "I can't have a man in my life who would restrict my freedom." Yet, playing with the pet parakeet that reminds her of her childhood garden, she wonders what she was meant to look like and whether plastic surgery could give her back her face.

"I feel ugly so many times, and I want to feel beautiful again as a woman," she says. "But I have to be strong for my family. I have to ensure that my sisters go to school. I want to have a home for my family. I want to become a lawyer to defend other women who have gone through injustice and fear for their lives."

Instinctively, Nadia turns the scarred side of her face from the camera.

I WANT TO HAVE THE FREEDOM OF BEING A MAN.

EVEN TODAY AS A WOMAN,

I CANNOT WALK MY MOTHER TO THE HOSPITAL

IN THE MIDDLE OF THE NIGHT

BY MYSELF.

—NADIA

Nadia and her pet bird.

Habiba at the compound where she lives with her two daughters.

HABIBA

There have been so many wars in Afghanistan that women rarely bother to specify in which war their loved ones died. Habiba's husband was killed by gunfire, though he wasn't a soldier. They had been married six years. He left her with two daughters, Lida, now 16, and Rashida, 12, born after his death.

With war raging in Kabul and ongoing disputes with her husband's family over land, Habiba decided to return to her village in the Kapisa region, when Rashida was a baby and Lida a small child. She had no money for transportation, so they joined a group of other families and walked. For 24 hours straight, they walked through desert. There was no water. Finally, they came to a stream and fell upon it, drinking like animals. A five-year-old boy drowned before anyone could save him. "He died of thirst," Habiba says.

In Kapisa, she and her daughters moved in with her brother-in-law, his wife, and their seven children. But life wasn't what she had hoped. Wars had so devastated the economy, there was no work. When news came that Taliban militants, fresh from war victories in Kabul, were heading for Kapisa, Habiba's family and many others fled in fear.

Again on foot, taking only what they could carry, the family trekked through the rugged province, overshadowed by the Hindu Kush mountains. Constantly in fear of getting caught by the Taliban, they were running at times in an effort to get to safety.

They settled in the Panjshir Valley, thought to be safe because of its towering mountains. Habiba, who was able to go to school as a child, quietly saw to it that her daughters learned to read and write. But she remained dependent on her brother-in-law. As soon as the Taliban fell, she fled again with her daughters, this time back to Kabul, where they moved in with her brother. She contributed a meager income to the household, mostly by weaving carpets that would pay them little, but cost a fortune abroad.

One day, seeking a better job, she walked to the Ministry of Women's Affairs in Kabul. There she heard about Women for Women International and signed up for a program in which she received courses in business and marketing skills, as well as women's rights training. Later, she applied for a position managing the organization's store in the *Bagh-e-Zenana,* the Women's Garden, in Kabul, a park and market area for women-run stores. Today she spends her days running the store, decorating it, keeping the books, and proudly chatting with customers.

She and her daughters live together in a single room. Adequate heating is rare in Kabul, and it is so cold that Lida, who washes their clothes, has to stop frequently to avoid frostbite from the ice water. Yet, both she and her sister smile. Lida says she hopes to become an English teacher. Rashida wants to be a computer scientist.

THERE WERE TIMES IN THE MIDST

OF OUR WALKING THAT SOMEONE WOULD YELL,

"THE TALIBAN ARE COMING!" AND WE WOULD ALL RUN FAST,

AS WE WERE AFRAID FOR OUR LIVES.

IF YOU FELL DURING THAT TIME, IT WAS HARD TO GET UP

AGAIN AS SO MANY PEOPLE WERE RUNNING.

—HABIBA
from Kabul

Habiba at the store she manages in the Bagh-e-Zenana in Kabul.

A muddy street, once the site of hand-to-hand combat, leads to Azada's home.

AZADA

In a world of much cruelty and little housing, children see everything.

"I endured the cruelty of my husband because I didn't have other choices," says Azada, 28. Her 10-year-old daughter Ramish, knowing the story, lays her head on her mother's shoulder. Her little sister, Benazira, listens.

A tea kettle sits on a small stove; in Afghan tradition, there is always tea, and the steam helps warm the freezing room. There is no running water, no real door. A makeshift curtain separates their room from the hallway, which leads to rooms of other families. On one wall is a picture of a religious figure; on the other, a drawing of an Indian film star, which would have been banned by the Taliban.

Like many Afghan women, Azada looks older than her years. She was married to a cousin at 14, not long after her family had fled war to live as refugees in Pakistan. Marriage to relatives is encouraged in Islam because it is believed relatives will treat their wives better than strangers. But it did not work out that way for Azada. She was his third wife. The owner of a car dealership, he went back and forth between wives in Pakistan and Afghanistan, abusing Azada whenever he came to town. She struggled to leave him, but had his two children to support.

"I married him because my father wanted me to," says Azada. "But I was also lucky enough to have a father who saved me."

Her father supported her decision to divorce and welcomed her and her daughters into his four-room house in Pakistan that was already home to her parents, two unmarried sisters, an unmarried brother, two married brothers, and the brothers' two wives and six children. Every family member worked day and night weaving carpets. The carpet dealer would give them the design and the wool. They received $50 for each carpet, which took two to three months to weave. To earn more, she took another job in a textile factory, walking 90 minutes each way. Community members derided her for leaving her husband and working outside the home. At night, she continued to weave.

After the Taliban fell, she and her family returned to Kabul, where she enrolled in gender-awareness classes and learned to cut semi-precious stones—work that was previously the domain of men. Today she teaches other women stone-cutting, beadwork, and design. Her most prized possession is her certificate of employment. "I never thought that one day I would have the opportunity to support myself without a man," she says. "Now I know I can do it. I am doing it!"

A curtain, instead of a door, separates Azada's family from another.

Azada's proud possession—her employment contract—as it fell on the carpet.

MARIGUL

Coming back from late afternoon prayers, Marigul comes alive when she talks about her situation. Her hands assume the gentle, open gestures of Islamic prayer. "I was praying for world peace," she says. The 50-year-old widow lives with her three sons in one small, cold room, the concrete floor covered with straw mats. Her married daughter lives elsewhere.

But didn't she want to pray for a better life, a higher income? She looks up with a smile. "I only prayed for world peace. We need peace. We are tired of wars," she says. Her children have never known a time of peace, and like most women in Afghanistan, she hopes for a brighter future for her offspring.

When her husband was killed in the war, and the Taliban took over, Marigul still had one advantage over some women: Her three sons could go outside the home, although she could not. But there was a limit to their endurance and fear, and eventually the family fled to Pakistan. "During the seven years we lived there, we faced many hardships. We survived by weaving carpets, and my sons learned making shoes," she says. When they returned to Afghanistan, they found their house destroyed, and they were dependent on the support of relatives.

A little over a year ago, Marigul enrolled in a program on women's rights and had a chance to talk for the first time with other women about experiences they had in common. After a year's vocational training, she obtained a microcredit loan to purchase raw materials and start a shoemaking business with her sons. The money also serves to rent a small shop. To help the struggling business against tough competition—Chinese manufacturers are flooding the market with inexpensive shoes—she works at home assembling shoeboxes.

With her new training and the beginning of a business, Marigul is hopeful that she can achieve stability and self-sufficiency for her family.

With gentle gestures, Marigul appeals for peace.

NOW THAT I HAVE ENROLLED MYSELF IN THIS ORGANIZATION, I AM VERY HAPPY. IT IS LIKE A DROP OF WATER THAT A PERSON POURS INTO THE MOUTH OF ANOTHER, WHO IS IN A DRY DESERT. THAT IS THE DROP OF WATER THAT IS GOING TO SAVE HER LIFE.

—KHALIDA

The one-room home of a family
of four (opposite) is heated by a small stove.
Marigul (left) assembles shoeboxes
for her new business.

دو ۴۶ ساعت حرف زیبا زدیم، نهار خوردیم. حال من و
خواهرانم در خانه مدرس کالا صنوعی ودکار مغازه کارا کلفم
مدرشتان لباسی زمستانی نداریم، اگر لباس داشته باشیم
یا پوشش نداریم، در هر حورت روز کار دست نقد میکو ری
شماره در مدرسه میم پردم تکلیف بعضی را راه و
کنه خودهن تکلیف کرده، کاد خودم مریض مالاریا گرفتم
میاشم کرده حل دعا معلم مدارپریک ای نیکو دی
خودهم کل میگویم درباره زندگی شما معلومات دلسگته باشم

DEAR KRISTY,

HELLO. HOW ARE YOU AND YOUR FAMILY?

I HOPE THIS LETTER FINDS YOU WELL AND HEALTHY. THANKS SO MUCH

FOR THE MONEY YOU HAVE SENT. I WANT TO BUY A SEWING MACHINE IN THE FUTURE.

I AM FROM PARWAN, A CITY IN AFGHANISTAN. DURING THE TALIBAN REGIME,

THEY BURNT OUR HOUSES, GARDENS, FARMS, AND NOW WE DON'T HAVE ANY PLACE TO LIVE IN.

AFTER THAT HORRIBLE EVENT, WE CAME TO KABUL WITH EMPTY HANDS.

WE STAYED IN A MOSQUE FOR ONE WEEK. THEN WE WENT TO A STRANGER'S HOUSE,

WE DID THEIR HOUSEWORK, SO THEY GAVE US A PLACE TO LIVE.

WE EVEN ATE FOOD THREE TIMES A WEEK. SOMETIMES ONCE IN 24 HOURS.

NOW I AND MY SISTERS WASH CLOTHES OR DO HOUSE CHORES IN HOUSES. WE DON'T HAVE WARM

CLOTHES FOR WINTER, IF WE FIND CLOTHES. WE DON'T HAVE SHOES TO WEAR.

MY FATHER HAS MENTAL PROBLEMS. MY SISTER HAS KIDNEY PROBLEMS.

I ALSO HAVE MALARIA. IT HURTS ME EVERY FOUR MONTHS.

—SHAHLA

A letter written in Dari to Shalah's American friend.

Noorzia with a letter from her sponsor.

NOORZIA

Noorzia is a woman in love: She is 40 years old and the mother of nine children. "What can I do?" she asks shyly. "My husband loves me so much!"

They live with her husband's parents, Nazuko and Moh, who are also devoted to each other. Once, when Taliban soldiers came to their door and demanded all their family's food, her father-in-law stood his ground and defied them, and soldiers began beating him. A second soldier raised his gun to shoot, and his wife Nazuko stepped in front of the gun to save him. His bullet grazed first her hand and then his ear. The fact that the family has a home at all is a blessing. During the war of Russian occupation, they had fled Kabul and lived in refugee camps in Pakistan that seemed to drain dignity from them one day at a time. "We depended on aid," she says. "It was tough having children and no shelter, no privacy, and no jobs to sustain you."

After nine years, they fled again, this time to Iran, where she and her husband and children found low-paying jobs and shared a house with her husband's first wife.

As soon as the war to remove the Taliban ended in 2001, they headed back to Kabul. This journey took six days. When they arrived, they found the city in rubble and their old house destroyed. There was little shelter. Families were sleeping in stores, in bombed-out buildings, and offices. The family moved into an abandoned house with a garden, but wonder when the owner will show up and evict them.

Noorzia enrolled in business-training classes and took out a small loan to start a restaurant she plans to develop into "a hotel for the poor." She cooks at home, her husband runs the restaurant, and her children help wash dishes when they're not in school. "I am a good cook," she says proudly. "I started the restaurant for my family's sake, but also to preserve our delicious Afghan food."

I SAID, "TALIBAN YOU CAN BEAT ME AND KILL ME, BUT DON'T HURT HIM." WHEN THE SOLDIE

Moh and his wife Nazuko.

ULLED THE TRIGGER, HIS BULLET NICKED MY HAND AND THEN HIS EAR.—NAZUKO

RESTAURANT-HOTEL

*A sagging roof and taped-up windows
bolster the small restaurant that Noorzia and her husband
established in this building. Patrons sit under the
eaves. "This is a restaurant for the poor," says one customer,
laughing. Inside is space for one bed, which
makes the establishment a hotel.*

At the women's center in Vardak province, once-isolated women gather for training and mutual support.

THE WOMEN'S CENTER

In Vardak province, one of Afghanistan's poorest areas, many men emigrated during the Taliban era to seek work. Only elderly men and young boys were allowed to move outside, or to do the shopping. Women could not leave the home.

Today women can move more freely in this conservative region, and they find great relief in getting together at the women's center, where they are learning about women's rights and engaging in literacy programs and practical training. Some women with established skills secure jobs to train other women.

Early on in the program, which began in 2002, one woman spoke up to say: "I have been here for four months, and I am learning about what is important in my life. I have found a community of women to support me, but I have only just realized that I have never once written my own name." The facilitator asked if other women, most of whom were illiterate, also wanted to write their names. The women all agreed, and by the end of the session each one had stood up and written her own name on the board.

The skills training covers an array of practical occupations, ranging from traditional crafts such as carpet weaving and knitting to making jams, jellies, and chutneys—not just for the home, but to sell in the marketplace or to supply bakeries, hotels, and stores. Other training includes hairstyling, along with giving manicures and pedicures. Jewelry-making involves the intricate skill of cutting semiprecious stones and designing artistic pieces. Following traditional patterns, women also decorate fabrics, belts, and hair ornaments with beads.

When the vocational skills training is successfully completed, the women take a basic business course to understand principles of accounting and creating a business plan so that they can take out a small loan to start their own businesses. Beyond the training, the women are happy to share their experiences and hopes for the future. Women normally meet only when there is a wedding party or other celebration in the village, otherwise there is little chance to get together.

They are all attaching great hopes on their children's future and want them to go to school. "Men have the opportunity to work outside the house. But we are here for our future," says one woman. "We do not want to see our daughters sit in the house and look for her brother's hand and income. From here on we are starting to bring changes to our families and to our society. We have to set examples for our daughters and pass on the idea that women are capable of doing whatever they want to do."

REWRITING HISTORY

During a discussion about women's roles, a girl stood up (opposite) and wrote on the board:

"Women. What about them?" One young woman shouted,

"Women in Afghanistan were ignorant, and now they are aware of their rights."

Another woman said, "I disagree with that. We always knew

what we wanted. We just never had the opportunity to express what we wanted.

The difference is, we can talk now, and we couldn't talk before."

Roughly cut beads of fluorite come in an array of colors for making jewelry (above). A young girl (opposite) shyly hides her face with fingers painted with nail polish that used to be taboo.

SUDAN

BEING A REFUGEE IS A TERRIBLE EXPERIENCE.

PEOPLE TREAT YOU LIKE YOU ARE NOTHING, LIKE YOU HAVE

NO VALUE IN THE WORLD.

—VICTORIA
originally from the Aweils

Photographs by Susan Meiselas

COUNTING MOONS

With arid deserts in the Arab north and tropical savannas in the tribal south, Sudan is as large and diverse as Western Europe. Defying easy answers, Sudan has spent its half century as an independent nation in violent struggle to find its own identity.

Most of Sudan's nearly 40 million people have known nothing but war. Two million people have died in civil war. Two generations of women have been raped as tools of war, and four million people have been uprooted from their homes. Khartoum is ringed with squalid camps full of refugees. They are war's victims, yet they are also its survivors. Counting the passage of time by new moons, many people traveled for months seeking safety. They walked through deserts and jungles, ate leaves to survive, and slept in trees to save their babies from being eaten by lions.

Sudan's cultural divides are steeped in bitter history—more than a thousand years of slavery, colonialism, and religious and ethnic differences. War has been waged largely to control the nation's riches: oil, gold, uranium, minerals, and arable land and scarce water. In 1955, a year before Sudan won independence from Britain

Previous pages: Sudanese refugees in Sinkat.

and Egypt, war erupted between the Khartoum-based government in the north and rebels in the south. Except for a decade-long break between 1972 and 1983, war has been endemic.

A parallel war broke out between rebels and government-sponsored militias in Sudan's western impoverished Darfur province in 2003. The government of Sudan armed and supported local tribal and other militias known as the *Janjaweed*, whose attacks on civilians have led to thousands of deaths and rapes.

Tribes in the eastern region—complaining of marginalization and lack of access to resources—riot periodically against government forces. Inter-tribal battles, wrenching famine, an influx of refugees from neighboring Ethiopia, Eritrea, and Chad, and murderous cross-border actions of Ugandan rebels present additional challenges.

The north-south war is generally characterized as a struggle between southern Sudanese with African tribal roots and those of ancestral Arab origin in the country's center and north. These lines are not clearly drawn, however, as migration has altered the composition of the country's population. Northern Sudan has been defined by cultural, economic, and political connections to Egypt and the Arab world, whereas southern Sudan has a stronger kinship with East African countries such as Kenya and Uganda. The north's comparative wealth owes much to the labor of southern slaves, brought northward by the north's merchant class starting hundreds of years before colonialism. Eventually these merchants exported slaves to the Middle East and the Americas. Slavery reemerged amid civil war in the late 1980s, as government militias seized thousands of southern Sudanese and forced them into labor and sexual servitude.

Colonialism cemented the north-south divide. British and Egyptian forces saw a ripe opportunity for land and resources in Sudan at the end of the 19th century and took Sudan under their control. Starting in 1899, Britain administered the north and south as two separate colonies. Arabic and English became official languages in the north, while English and languages representing major tribes, including Dinka, Nuer, Bari, and Shilluk, were the south's official languages. The British developed the north's economy and infrastructure, and the south continued in its tribal ways. Yet in 1946, Britain succumbed to pressure from the northern elite to unite the two areas. Arabic became the official language in the south, although it had never been spoken

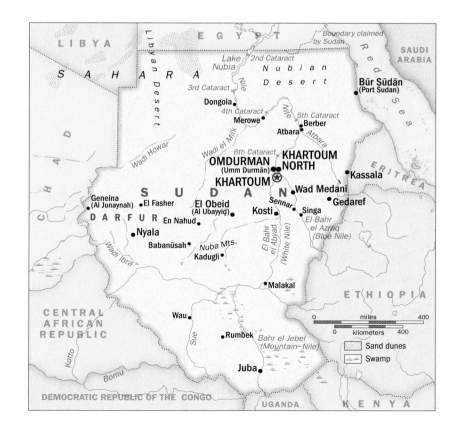

there, and northern administrators assumed positions of influence. Resentment brewed as southerners felt shut out of the new government and resisted the imposition of the Arabic language. When the British vacated about 800 government posts in advance of independence, almost none went to southerners.

The Khartoum government never made good on promises to carve out a place for southerners in the postcolonial administration. Southern anger turned to violence against administrators from the north, sparking the beginnings of civil war. The government relied on the aid from several countries at various times during the war, including the former Soviet Union, Egypt, China, and the United States, each eager to promote their own interests in the region. The discovery of oil in commercial quantities in the south in the late 1970s raised the stakes of conflict higher, as southerners resisted government attempts to redefine the country's boundaries and cut them off from oil wealth. In 1983, southern army members formed a major rebel group called the Sudan People's Liberation Army. In 1991, this group split into factions bringing forth new waves of violence. In the same year, the government instituted a new penal code, which attempted to institute a strict interpretation of Islamic law to govern the lives of Christians and adherents to traditional African faiths.

Civilian suffering throughout these years of war defies the imagination. Survivors tell stories of militias storming villages in the dead of night, setting homes on fire, and shooting family and friends. Rebels gang-raped women and kidnapped boys to become soldiers and girls to serve as sex slaves. They stole cattle and every item of value they found. Those who were lucky to escape faced treacherous journeys to relative safety. Upon reaching camps within Sudan or in neighboring countries, survivors entered a new world of desperation. Many camps overflowed with human suffering, as starvation and disease took children from parents and left children orphaned. Women lived in fear of nightly rape and sexual torture.

A peace agreement signed in January 2005 between the southern rebels and the central government gave the south autonomy for six years. Southern Sudanese will vote in 2011 on whether to remain united with northern Sudan or secede and form their own nation. Profits from oil are meant to be shared equally between the north and south.

Women face enormous obstacles in addition to the challenges of recovering from war. In 2005, it was more likely that a girl born in southern Sudan would die from a pregnancy-related complication than complete primary school: One in nine women dies during pregnancy or childbirth, yet only one in a hundred girls completes primary school. Traditional female genital cutting is practiced at one of the highest rates in the world, and early and forced marriage are both common.

Accounts of the turmoil of war have shed little light on women's proud history or the organized networks piloted by women across class lines to alleviate suffering. Compared to other countries in the region, women have played an important role in public life and have been active in the workforce. As early as the 1940s, women began creating organizations to promote their rights. One leading group, the Sudanese Women's Union, won the right for women to vote in 1953. One of the founders of the group later became the first female member of parliament. Women have created women's universities and crafted a sophisticated women's studies curriculum. Grassroots organizations teach women in prison and help them understand their rights. Others have created programs to convince tribal chiefs to let girls finish school.

Long barred from returning to their home, Sudanese are beginning to flow south. Some will return to areas where not a single building stands. Women make up about 60 percent of this population; they are forming groups to cultivate the land—work normally done by men—and figure out how to get access to land. One organization is giving seeds, tools, and goats to women and teaching them how to earn extra income. When these women have grown roots in their new home and have something left over to share, they plan to repay in kind with the fruits of their labor.

كان لدينا مزرعة كبيرة وبيت كبير أيضا كان لي وأمي ترعوذ
قرية جميع احتفالات البلدية و القرية كان منزل رفع وقب
عاصمة الحبش كان عنده ٨٥٨ رأس من الغنم و ١٩ رأس من
البقر كنا علينا نأخذهم إلى الخلاء ، للأكل الفش وشرب الماء من
الجداول كانت حياتنا في فرح ومرح شديد دون أن نعرف يوم من الأيام
سوف تكون حرب في السودان .

لقد بدأ العرب يدخل في قتل غنم و خالق الذلو عرفنا أن
يوم يدخل من أسرتنا يموت خالق وعم في نفس الوقت كان
موتهم صعوبة لدى الأسرة لفقدهم من الأسرة الذلو
عرفنا أن العرب بدأ حادة مع الدينكا وفعلا العرب العربية بدأ
تقتل بيتنا بسرعة شديدة كل يوم بعد يوم وفعل وقفت صياح
الناس من قبل العمل .

WE HAD A HERD OF 38 GOATS AND 19 COWS.

I USED TO TAKE THEM FOR GRAZING ALONG WITH MY NEPHEW, SIMON.

I WAS HAPPY AND INNOCENT. BUT LITTLE BY LITTLE THE WAR

STARTED CREEPING INTO MY LIFE TO EVENTUALLY SHAPE MY FUTURE.

THE FIRST DIRECT STRIKE CAME WHEN MY UNCLE AND MY COUSINS'

FAMILIES WERE KILLED DURING THE ATTACK OF LIRI EAST IN 1985. I FELT THE LOSS

DEEPLY…. WAR WAS RAPIDLY AND NONDISCRIMINATELY SPREADING

LIKE FIRE THROUGHOUT SOUTHERN SUDAN.

—KARAK
from the Nuba Mountains

A letter written in Arabic from Karak to her American sponsor.

KARAK

Karak is a working mother. Moving through throngs of people in displaced persons camps, wide with open sewage trenches and hopelessness, she is besieged by requests for advice. People put questions to her and listen for her answers. She is determined, a woman with unquestioned strength and a vision of the future.

At home a few hours later that day, Karak acknowledges that she feels a sense of surrender in her personal life. She teaches her children to read, while her husband glowers, resentful of her standing in her community and independence. She has lost countless family members to reasons stemming from war. Her sister recently died of AIDS after being forced into prostitution in displaced persons camps.

"My husband wants me to stay home with the children, but I can't," she says. "I am saving myself in the process as well. I can't see other girls going through what my sister went through. I have to be there for them."

Karak was born in 1977 in the Nuba Mountains, near al-Wahda. Her mother is Christian and her father Muslim. They are members of an ethnic minority called the Upper Nile Dinkas. Thousands of Dinkas have been killed in Sudan's shifting war over resources, power, and tribal rivalries. "I always felt chased by people I didn't know, for reasons I didn't understand," she says.

She and her family have often been divided by war and circumstance. She was seven when her father took her to another place to live with an uncle and cousins. She learned to love this family and was put in charge of keeping the cattle. "I was happy and innocent," she remembers. "We had a herd of 38 goats and 19 cows." Then her uncle and cousins were massacred. Her family joined her, but when she came back from grazing one day, she found her mother and siblings sobbing helplessly. Her father had been kidnapped. "Without thinking, I ran to the police station, thinking that they would help me save my father.

Karak is surrounded by women asking her advice in one of the displaced persons camps that ring Khartoum.

> IF SOMETHING ISN'T DONE,
> IT WILL BE EASY TO USE
> "CULTURE" AS A REASON FOR
> LIMITING WOMEN'S ACCESS TO
> THE DECISION-MAKING
> PROCESS AND EVOLVING AS
> HUMAN BEINGS IN ORDER TO
> ENSURE THE FULL DEVELOPMENT
> OF SUDANESE SOCIETY.
>
> —KARAK
> *now a resident of Rumbek*

As I was running, I fell and got up blindly many times, running again, tears blocking my eyes, and sadness filling my heart," she says.

She found her father on the way. He and other Dinka men had been rounded up by soldiers. Her father whispered to her to leave. She refused. "I preferred to stay and die with him if necessary," she says. Soldiers began whipping her as she clung to him. They loaded them both onto a truck jammed with other people. "We were no longer hearing their shouts, nor feeling their whips, but listening to the fast beats of our own hearts," she says.

They were saved by a military officer who arrived to deliver the soldiers' paychecks. A spell of rage engulfed the officer when soldiers told him they were supposed to take them to Kadogli, but would slaughter them on the way. "These are innocents!" he shouted, forcing open the truck door. Karak's father took her hand, and they ran.

Later, soldiers threatened her father. Homes were burned. Their precious cattle were stolen. Finally, they fled. Impoverished, her mother made the ultimate sacrifice: To educate her daughters, she split them up and sent them away, each to a different family. Karak was educated, but her sister was less fortunate. "They were better off financially and treated me well," she says of the family that took her in. "But why does life have to be about such choices?"

Karak quickly rose to the top of her class and pinned her salvation on a college education. At night, she struggled with loneliness, as she moved from one relative's house to the next, fleeing first an abusive aunt, then an uncle who tried to marry her off. By the time she graduated from high school, she felt lucky to be living in a displaced persons camp in Khartoum with a stipend to help her through school. Her family joined her, and her small stipend helped support them all. Then the camp was demolished. Her father took seriously ill. To pay his hospital bills, she began cleaning houses and lost her place at university.

She wound up in a clerical job, where she met a teacher who wanted to marry her. After making him promise she could attend university, she agreed. They were married in 1995 in Dar Es Salaam Mandela Camp. After the wedding, he balked at her going to university. She gave birth to three children.

Karak began volunteering at a primary school and taught evening classes to women. The International Rescue Committee (IRC) recruited her as a literacy teacher for a women's empowerment program. She joined training workshops and became a consultant in conflict resolution. At night, she went to Juba University and graduated with a degree in Gender and Development. She started her own nonprofit organization, the Friendship Agency for Community Training (FACT).

Not long after these photographs were taken, Karak became Women for Women International's first staff member in Sudan and left her husband to start operations in Rumbek. Her mother lives with her and helps care for the children.

"With the peace agreement now in place, I want to help southerners to come back and help to rebuild south Sudan," she says. "There is so much to be done to make sure that women are not continually left behind. If something isn't done, it will be easy to use 'culture' as a reason for limiting women's access to the decision-making process and evolving as human beings in order to ensure the full development of Sudanese society."

*Karak at home,
with her son (opposite).
Karak teaches her
children to read and
write English (left).*

ABU GHRAIB

A woman digs for dry dirt in an unofficial displaced persons

camp that becomes so flooded in rain that residents sleep

in shifts. The camp (opposite) was built by thousands of migrants who

settled here, quilting tents out of scraps of donated fabric, because

they could not gain entry to official refugee camps beyond.

When officials found out about the camp, they surrounded it with barbed wire.

"Look at us," says one resident, referring to the infamous Iraqi prison

that has become the camp's unofficial name.

"We live in Abu Ghraib."

CATTLE CAMPS

The Dinka are the largest tribe in Sudan. For generations, the Dinka lived in seasonal cattle camps. Along with other southern tribes, they measure their wealth and identity in cattle. They have more than a hundred terms to differentiate cows by their shape, color, and behavior. Children grow up learning to sing praise to bulls, cure hides, and milk cows. Girls grow up coloring their hair with cow urine. Boys make medicines of cow dung to cover wounds.

Girls and boys meet while tending cattle. Their marriages are sealed in cattle contracts; cattle with the most elaborate horns are often given as dowries. When a girl marries, cows are given not to her, but to her family; property is passed through the paternal line. Women's lives are dictated by the terms of these contracts.

If a woman wants a divorce before having children, her family must repay her husband's family a 10 percent bonus in cows. If she wants to leave after bearing a child, the penalty is adjusted, and the child stays with the father. If her husband dies, she is inherited by male family members. A son must consummate marriage with all his father's wives except his mother. Lacking the cows to buy divorces, many women remain in abusive marriages.

Sudan's 21-year-old war has both interrupted and reinforced these traditional practices. Women were seen as booty to be taken and enslaved. Without husbands to protect them, Dinka women have faced rape by both Arab militia and opposing tribesmen. Once they arrive in displaced persons camps, many are victimized again.

"This is your husband; you just keep quiet and endure," the manager of one Internally Displaced Persons (IDP) camp told a woman who complained. "This has not happened only to you, it happened to many women here. You see those women here in the camp with the men. These are their new husbands."

Today, cattle camps themselves are at a crossroad. Children play a critical role in the agricultural economy. Parents face a choice between educating their children and feeding them. Only a third of south Sudan's population is believed to be literate, and adolescents increasingly gravitate to cities.

South Sudan has never had much infrastructure; electricity, drinking water, and health-care systems barely exist in many parts of the region. After years of war, roads leading to villages are pocked with hidden land mines. Yet, because of peace agreements and recently discovered oil reserves in the south, the southerners' hopes are high. In early 2006, nearly 5,000 displaced Dinka returned to the southern town of Bor under the auspices of international organizations. Dinka men drove hundreds of thousands of cattle down the east bank of the Nile on foot. Meanwhile, women, children, and the aged were boarded onto ferries. When they disembarked, they were singing.

Dinka women and children are charged with tending cattle, which makes them a target of marauding militia.

187

Upon marrying, a girl's
family receives cows
as her dowry. A tall girl
may bring 150 cows,
a short girl just 30.

PLOMIA

Until she was married, Victoria spent most of her life walking. She is 23. She was five years old when her Dinka village was attacked by the *Murahaleen*, militia backed by the Khartoum government. The militia rounded up all the men, put them inside the *lak*—their cattle barn—and set the barn on fire.

"My husband was inside—he was burning alive, I could smell the flesh," says her mother, Plomia, 45. "We were not allowed to cry—if you cried, they would shoot you. Instead, they made us dance. They would force us to dance and force us to stop. Those of us who danced would be allowed to be with our children." The Murahaleen also destroyed their crops, slaughtered their cattle, and raped young women or sold them into Sudan's slave trade. But Plomia's family escaped.

"We started walking, me and my children, in hunger, misery, and fear," she says. "I had nothing—I was not even wearing any clothes." There was no food, so they ate leaves. There was no water, so they drank from animal ponds. Domesticated animals, newly terrified of humans with guns, fled from them as they walked.

Three months later—Plomia counted the moons—they arrived in the city of Rumbek. But civil war between the government in the largely Arab north and rebel fighters in the tribal and black African south had spread. Inquiring, she heard there was hunger in Uganda, but safety in Ethiopia. So she found a boat ride across the Nile and spent three days crossing crocodile-infested waters with her children. Once in Ethiopia, they were given food and shelter at a refugee camp run by the Sudan People's Liberation Army. Six months later, the camp was burned down by Ethiopian rebels.

They fled with other refugees to Uganda. Many people died along the way—from hunger, drowning, or Sudanese government bombs. Plomia and her children made it alive and were ultimately admitted into a relief camp. When Ugandan rebels bombed the camp, they headed back to Sudan. They were living in Rumbek when peace accords were signed. They wanted to return to their village to visit, but Victoria was no longer free to travel; her husband, who had agreed to give 30 cows as part of her dowry, would not allow it. Plomia sold the first 10 cows to pay her brother's school fees. When the husband pays the remaining 20, those cows will go to help pay the dowry for her brother's wife.

"That is our culture, unfortunately," says Plomia.

PRESCILLA

Prescilla, 45, is the first of her husband's nine wives. Like women in many areas emerging from war, she has taken on leadership roles that women in traditional patriarchal societies are rarely permitted to play. After her husband died, she became the head of a large family clan, a successful businesswoman, and a recognized political leader.

A member of the Dinka Agar, she was a fighter, even as a girl. She used to help her mother distribute food to local soldiers fighting government militia. She witnessed her mother's death on the battlefield and went back the next day to carry on her mother's work. This, she says, was her form of contributing to the war against the government-backed militia.

Her husband, an officer in the Sudan People's Liberation Army, died in battle. They had nine children. As the first wife, she inherited responsibility for the other wives after his death. She also took responsibility for her dead brothers' wives, her daughters, many children, and others in need. People turn to her for shelter, for food, and for counsel in making decisions involving both women and men. Active in politics, she has been named by the government of south Sudan as "Woman Leader of Akot County."

Her cane, the consequence of legs broken en route to a conference, has become a sign of her standing in the community.

Prescilla is also a hardheaded businesswoman, the owner of five stores and a restaurant. She believes women must own businesses to be independent. She travels and incorporates modern conveniences into her spotless traditional compound. "Economic progress will be what gives us the freedom, the freedom to care for our children and educate our children," she says.

Living in a society that accords women little respect, she is determined to change attitudes toward women. "Women need training and education if we are going to move Sudan to peace and stability," she says. "I am determined to do my part for my family, my daughters, my children, and the other women that I see everyday who continue to suffer."

Several of her own six daughters were married and mistreated and have returned to live with her. She is happy to have them back to continue their education. "As women, we have to be delicately tough," she says. "I'm teaching my daughters and granddaughters the balancing act of being a woman in Dinka culture."

"Don't make friendship with credit. Come tomorrow," says the sign at Prescilla's store. *"We are still going on, if God wills. New Sudan."*

Prescilla, a Dinka matriarch, in her living compound (above). Family members share cooking chores (opposite).

ONCE THEY HAVE PAID COWS FOR YOUR DAUGHTER, THEY OWN HER....

AS WOMEN WE HAVE TO BE DELICATELY TOUGH.

I'M TEACHING MY DAUGHTERS AND GRANDDAUGHTERS THE BALANCING ACT

OF BEING A WOMAN IN DINKA CULTURE.

—PRESCILLA
from Rumbek

PAYING FOR PASSAGE

When she fled for safety
with other women and their children,
Nybel, shown tending the pan,
put all her clothing on her body.
She paid one layer of clothing to a ferryman,
another to cross a road, and
others to buy food. By the time she arrived in
Rumbek a month later, she was wearing
only a bra and a skirt. She is surrounded at the
camp by others from her village.

BEJA WOMEN

Outside Port Sudan, these Beja women
emerge from a class on women's rights. The Beja, a mix
of ancient Red Sea tribes, are traditionally
nomadic and independent. Federal
dams have cut their water supply and escalated conflict.
Children in Beja tent communities travel up to
an hour each way for water.

LITERACY CLASS

*Mariam, a Beja woman (right), points
to a drawing on a blackboard in a literacy class
taught by the Abu Hadia Association
outside Port Sudan. Literacy among women in
the nomadic tribes is low.
The classes, which also educate women
about female genital cutting, persuaded
her to stop the traditional practice
on her daughters. Mariam (opposite) stands
just outside the classroom.*

Stones mark a school assembly area (opposite). Women and children (above) walk or ride for hours to fetch water.

FATIMA

Women are not allowed to walk alone in public in Fatima's conservative Beja culture. She does so anyway as an act of civil disobedience. Almost completely shrouded by clothing—even her hands are covered—she goes about running her businesses. Men do not challenge her. In fact, they seem mesmerized.

Fatima identifies herself as an "Islamic capitalist." She started two small businesses, including a grain mill. The businesses, managed by her brothers, support her work as a grassroots political organizer and teacher of women's rights to other Beja women in Port Sudan.

Port Sudan, on the Red Sea, is surrounded by unforgiving desert and soaring heat in summer. It is home to 250,000 internally displaced persons from warfronts in the south, from Darfur in the west, and from neighboring Eritrea. It is the hub of the Beja people, ancient tribes that follow conservative Islamic customs. Girls memorize the Koran, but are rarely taught to read. Lack of education virtually assures they will undergo female genital excision and marry at an early age.

Fatima is an indefatigable advocate of both women's rights and the culture that limits them. Her association is one of several vibrant civil organizations in the Port Sudan area dedicated to helping improve the lot of marginalized women. There is a small women's university in Port Sudan, a legal rights organization, and a handful of schools, some founded by men.

The region is beset by periodic violence among various tribes and ongoing battles between Beja tribes and the Khartoum government over access to resources and representation. Dams built by the federal government in Khartoum have stolen water the Beja people need to live. Fatima yearns to make Americans as aware of the plight of the Beja as they are of the victims of war to the west in Darfur. The United States, she says, is the "land that brings freedom and democracy to people."

She vows: "If no one pays attention to us and our demands, we will fight until we bring attention to ourselves as the Darfurians have."

Fatima, center, teaches English after school.

GRINDING GRAIN

*Fatima explains operations
at a mill, which her brothers run.
Profits from the mill
help underwrite the costs of her
women's programs.*

Members of Fatima's association dance in celebration, after they read the Koran and discuss women's rights. Their movements simulate camels walking.

MODERN CONVENIENCES

Fatima's life is different from that of most Beja women.

She left her fiancé for ideological reasons and lives with her family.

Her mother, who does not approve of her lifestyle,

takes charge of all household duties. Fatima does not even know

how to make coffee, yet she purchased everything

for this household with the income from her businesses—including

the satellite dish in the back yard. "I wanted to know what was going on

in the world," she says. She tunes in to CNN.

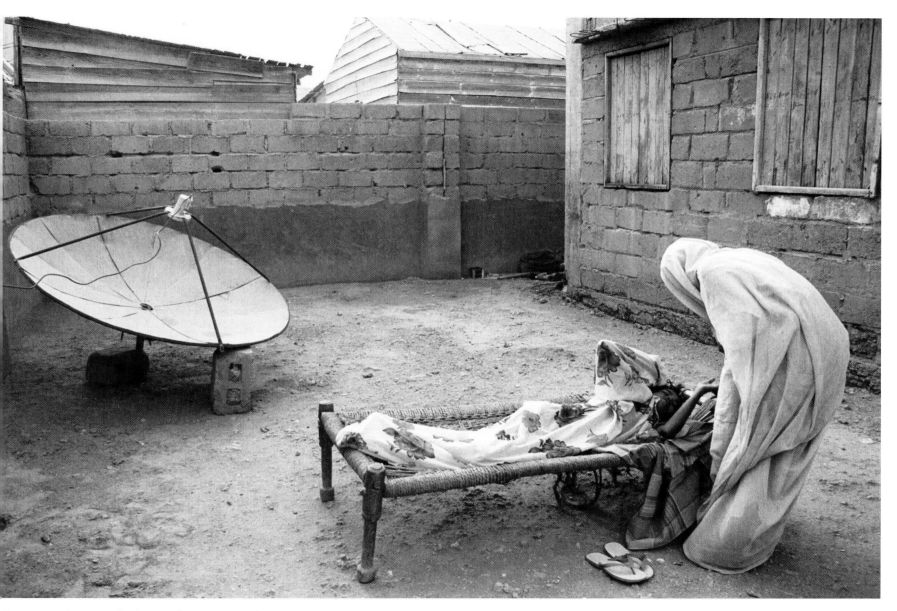

Fatima rouses her sister, who slept outside, to start a new day.

Houaida, wearing the white of a professional woman, explains different types of female genital cutting.

WOMEN'S LEGAL AWARENESS GROUP

It is 120°F in the desert. There is no sign of water, just a tent off the road. Inside, a teacher stands by an easel with a chart outlining women's inheritance rights. Her students, a mix of local Beja women and other women forced from their villages by war, are mostly illiterate. They listen intently and display great energy. The instructor, who wears the white clothing that denotes a professional degree, is seven months pregnant. Her name is Houaida.

She is a cofounder of the Women's Legal Awareness Group, a grassroots group founded in 1998 by women lawyers who realized that many marginalized women displaced by war were being imprisoned without access to legal counsel. The organization offers legal training and representation to women around Port Sudan.

"How long must a man provide housing for a wife after divorce?" a woman swathed in yellow asks Houaida. "For three months, or three menstrual cycles, if she doesn't have children," she answers, explaining that within three months, she will know whether she is pregnant. What about beating? Sudanese law distinguishes between legal disciplinary hitting and illegal violent hitting, she explains, adding that the law distinguishes the two according to tools used, marks left, and parts of the body struck.

Sudanese law is based on the government's interpretation of Islamic Sharia, or family law. Single men and women can be whipped 80 times for extramarital affairs. A married woman who has an extramarital affair can be stoned to death. Rapists are subject to one hundred lashes and ten years in prison.

But Port Sudan is filled with thousands of women, including many widows and single heads of households, who are not Muslim; they have fled war in the largely Christian and animist south. According to the association, most of the women in the prison system are single heads of household far from their homes. With no way to support their children, many brew beer, a traditional form of generating income. In Sudan's conservative Islamic east, they are jailed for three to six months for violating laws that prohibit the sale of alcohol. If they cannot make bail, their children often go to prison with them.

"We need to acknowledge that Sudanese society is diverse and does not have only Muslims in it," says Houaida, who is Muslim. "The law must protect those who are not Muslims, too."

The organization also lobbies to change laws that adversely impact women, such as a requirement that it takes the testimony of two women witnesses to equal the weight of a single male witness.

GUARD

*A woman guard in Port Sudan
prison is charged with watching female prisoners.
Many of her prisoners are internally
displaced persons from other
regions who are jailed for brewing beer
to earn money to feed their families.*

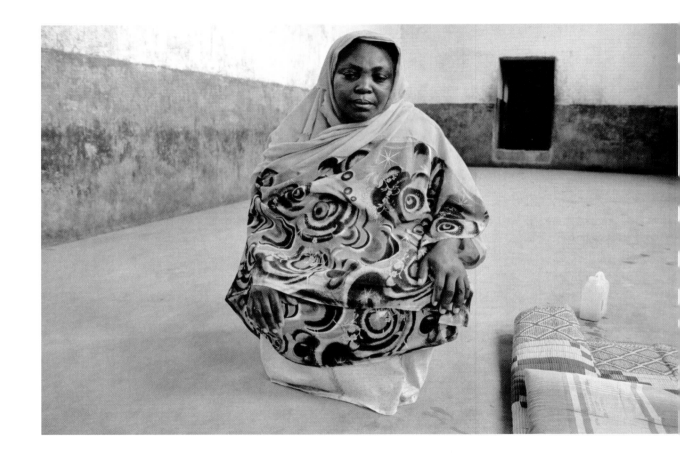

PRISONER

The mother of three is serving time with
her children for brewing beer.
Sudanese laws against selling alcohol are
strictly enforced in Islamic areas around Port Sudan,
but not in her native southern Sudan.
Men who buy beer are not punished.

SOUTHERN WOMEN'S ASSOCIATION

Forty southern women living in a camp in eastern Sudan

have organized and elected officers to improve their desperate living conditions.

A treasurer keeps track of funds they raise by sewing and

crocheting. War is intolerant of handicaps. Yet, even in war, there is

kindness. At center is a mute woman, a mother of four,

who is supported by the others. In Sudanese

society, when a mute woman raises her hand, others

immediately stop talking to help her.

BRIDES OF PORT SUDAN

The Good Association, started by middle-class
teachers, helps marginalized women learn to make banners
that are used as dowries and wedding decorations.
In Beja culture, dowries go to women
and today may include boom boxes and camels.
Women often sell camels to buy jewelry or gold
as a financial nest egg.

RWANDA

WHEN THE CONFLICT STARTED,

IT MADE NO SENSE TO ANY OF US.

WE DID NOT CONSIDER EACH OTHER AS ENEMIES.

WE WERE INTERMARRIED.

WE LIVED THE SAME LIFE.

—BEATA

Photographs by Sylvia Plachy

THE CHILDREN FORGOT TO CRY

Genocide came cheap. The machetes, some 500,000 of them, had been imported from China. The small arms for the military came mostly from European suppliers, many bought with international loans. It was the hate that was costly: During a span of 100 days in 1994, about 800,000 people were slaughtered.

Rwanda is a tiny, landlocked country, surrounded by Burundi, the Democratic Republic of the Congo, Uganda, and Tanzania. Rwanda's gentle slopes, covered with banana trees, have earned it the name "land of a thousand hills." One of the most densely populated countries in Africa, it is nonetheless largely rural. Clusters of mud huts dot the hillsides, where 90 percent of the population farms the land, known since colonial days for its yields of coffee and tea.

In 1895, Rwanda became part of German East Africa, but continued to be governed by a Tutsi king. After Germany lost World War I, Belgium took control. As was the case in the Congo, Belgian policies took a harsh toll and helped lay the groundwork for future ethnic strife. An identity card forced people to assert whether they were Hutu

Previous pages: Machete

or Tutsi, groups based more on class than ethnic divisions. Although many positions of influence were held by the Tutsi, most Tutsi were cattle holders. Hutu farmed the land; by acquiring measures of stature, a Hutu could become a Tutsi. Centuries of intermarriage had made it difficult to distinguish the groups by physical features. Belgium decreed that those with ten or more cows would be Tutsi.

Belgian governors cultivated Tutsi elites into a new social class, motivated by a perception that they had more "European" features and were more fit to govern. Belgium established schools to educate Tutsi sons to serve as government personnel, but denied Hutu children an education beyond primary school. Traditional Tutsi hill chiefs served as enforcers, collecting taxes and inflicting corporal punishment on Hutu. Suspicion and distrust replaced the ancient social contracts.

Belated proposals to democratize the system in the 1950s, forwarded in part by Belgians and members of the Hutu elite educated in seminary schools, were met with opposition from the Tutsi elite, leading to a Hutu revolt that overthrew the Tutsi king in 1959. A Hutu government was elected in a UN-supervised election, and Rwanda was granted its independence in 1962. Hutu majority rule ushered in a wake of violence. About 20,000 Tutsi were killed, and 150,000 were driven into exile. Large-scale violence occurred again in 1964 and 1974. Domestic and international attempts to address the political issues were undermined by corruption and festering social ills.

Maj. Gen. Juvenal Habyarimana, a Hutu, took power via a military coup in 1973 and was elected president by a large majority in 1978. Over the next two decades, he developed an entrenched one-party system that would prove capable of instigating genocide-on-command. Spurred by some reforms, Habyarimana received significant foreign aid. Rwanda's level of debt soared between 1976 and 1994, and Habyarimana siphoned off aid for his personal use. Using rhetoric later compared to Cambodia's Pol Pot, Habyarimana extolled manual labor and kept Rwanda's peasants poor and uneducated in the name of producing food. They had to give one day of unpaid labor—*umuganda*—each week for various projects, a policy that gave the regime experience in mobilizing peasants to "act as one."

The nation's lasting poverty was blamed on unproductive urban intellectuals: the Tutsi. Discrimination against Tutsi women increased. In 1990 a newspaper published the "Hutu Ten Commandments,"

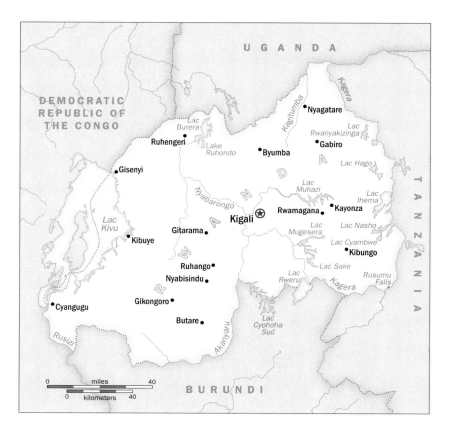

condemning anyone who maintained a relationship with a Tutsi woman and extolling the virtues of Hutu women. Yet, it was reported that at least a fifth of all Rwandan women experienced domestic abuse.

Amid growing corruption, President Habyarimana's popularity waned and opposition to his rule gathered among the Tutsi diaspora living in exile in neighboring countries, as well as among moderate Hutu. In 1990 the Tutsi-led Rwandan Patriotic Front (RPF), launched an offensive in Rwanda. The increasing instability led to a ceasefire in 1991 between the government, the RPF, and other opposition groups. A peace agreement—the Arusha Accords—was signed in 1993 and included measures to establish a democratic government. Yet the government and Hutu militia groups were preparing for genocide at the same time that peace was being negotiated.

On April 6, 1994, Habyarimana and the president of Burundi were killed when their plane was shot down as it prepared to land in Kigali. Within 45 minutes of the crash, an attack on the country's Tutsi and moderate Hutu began. The killing was organized at the highest levels of government and carried out by members at all levels of society, especially by poor, unemployed young men enticed with money, food, and alcohol to join militias known as *Interahamwe*. For three months, Rwanda's bucolic countryside was transformed into killing fields as public broadcasts called for umuganda to exterminate the Tutsi. Using lists and identity cards, perpetrators tortured and murdered innocents, neighbors, and sometimes their own family members. Failure to

participate in the killing could be its own death warrant. An estimated 250,000 to 500,000 women were raped in three months—many after being forced to watch the murder of family members. Some were also mutilated, tortured, and purposely infected with HIV.

The slaughter was witnessed on the world stage almost in real time through news reports. Many blamed the international community for not intervening to stop the genocide. After the murder of 10 Belgian peacekeepers, about 2,500 UN peacekeepers were evacuated during the massacres, and only 200 were allowed to remain. This small group led by Lt. Gen. Roméo Dallaire was forbidden to use weapons. The UN rejected Dallaire's pleas for backup and authority to act defensively on behalf of the population. The RPF finally defeated the Hutu, but during the intervening hundred days, an estimated 800,000 Tutsi and moderate Hutu were killed. Fearing retribution, at least two million Hutu refugees, including militia members responsible for much of the genocide, fled to neighboring countries.

The war officially ended on July 16, 1994. The RPF helped form Rwanda's transitional Government of National Unity, and the international community began relief operations. Even the aid was fraught with controversy as portions were directed to refugee camps in Congo, which housed many of those responsible for the genocide.

The International Criminal Tribunal for Rwanda served as a milestone for bringing violence against women in war to international attention, in large part due to intense activism by survivors and women's advocacy groups. For the first time in history, an international court made the decision to consider rape and sexual enslavement as crimes against humanity. In 1998, the panel convicted a former mayor of nine counts of genocide and crimes against humanity, including rape. Rape was also made a first-degree crime in Rwanda's local courts.

The historic tragedy triggered improbable social change. At war's end, so many men had died or fled that 70 percent of the population was female. Widows dealing with enormous trauma became their families' sole breadwinners and took on labor only men had done before. Left to put their shattered country back together, women had to bridge their differences and work side by side with neighbors whose relatives had killed members of their family. Together they carried bricks and built houses to replace the thousands that had been burned to the ground. They took in each other's children and found homes for some of the 500,000 orphans from the war. In every province, groups formed to help widows and refugees returning to the country.

To move forward, it was in Rwanda's national interest to empower its women. Historically, Rwandese women needed their husband's permission to engage in any type of economic activity. They were not eligible for loans or credit. They could not inherit land or property, even after the death of their husband. After the war, women began to speak out for rights and equality. Delegates sent to the Fourth World Conference on Women in Beijing in 1995 returned energized to build a strong women's movement. Women in civil organizations campaigned

to improve the status of women. Their efforts resonated with the transitional government, some of whose members had witnessed successful efforts to expand the role of women in politics in Uganda.

Laws were rewritten to give women new social, legal, and economic rights. Women first served on the drafting committee and then worked with local organizations to make sure that every level of Rwandan society understood what was in the constitution before a vote was held; of the constitution's main articles 22 reflected a commitment to equality between men and women, including a statement that men and women shared responsibility for family. The new constitution was adopted by public referendum in June 2003.

A critical provision in the constitution reserves 24 of the 80 seats in parliament for women. When elections were held, officially ending the nine-year post-genocide transition period, just over 49 percent of all representatives in the new parliament were women. The country gave women not only more seats in parliament than they had been guaranteed under the constitution, but a more equitable percentage of seats in parliament than any other nation on Earth.

It will take years for gains at the national level to make a difference in the lives of ordinary women, especially in remote areas. But the changes have already inspired women at all levels of society. "I want the women of Rwanda, from the rural poor to the urban elite, to be independent, to be educated," said Solange Tuyisenge, 32, after she was elected to the legislature. "I want them to become peacemakers."

THE FLIGHT

During the genocide, this road (right)—
leading from the Rwandan town of Gisenyi
to the border city of Goma in the
Democratic Republic of the Congo—was filled
with throngs of people trying to flee the massacre.
Many never made it across the border
and were thrown into the Nyabarongo River.
Steers (opposite) are being
herded before daylight toward grazing
pastures in Ruhengeri.

FROM THE SHALLOWS

Like many women,
Rosine, a Tutsi, had to watch as her husband
was killed before her eyes.
Then, after being severely beaten,
she and her two daughters were taken to a lake
with dozens of others and thrown
into the water to drown.
They were the only survivors.

ON THE SURFACE, IF YOU ARE LOOKIN

T MY MORPHOLOGY, I COULD PASS AS A HUTU. I TRIED, BUT THE INTERAHAMWE...

...DID NOT BELIEVE ME.—ROSINE

ROSINE

It was still in the early days of the genocide when the *Interahamwe* came and killed Rosine's husband in front of her. She tried to escape, but they caught her. Then, they examined her for the fine ethnic distinctions that they thought would be able to tell them for certain whether she was Tutsi or Hutu.

"On the surface, if you are looking at my morphology, I could pass as a Hutu," she says. "I tried to, but they did not believe me."

They examined her skin. It was too soft for a Hutu, they said. They felt her hair between their fingers and told her it was too silky, too fine for a Hutu. Then they started beating her and took her and her two small daughters away with dozens of others to Lake Muhazi.

"There were about 62 of us; they took and threw into the lake," she says. "Only three people survived. Those three people were me and my two girls. When they threw us in the lake, we were dropped on the side in shallow water. I managed to get out of the water and run with the children to hide in the bushes."

A kindly man gave them shelter. But Rosine was so badly beaten about the head that she suffered permanent trauma. Except for her daughters, she lost her entire family. The slaughter she had witnessed drove her nearly crazy. "At one point, I was so traumatized that I almost committed suicide," she says. "I did not want to cope with living." She went on for the sake of her daughters.

After the Rwandan Patriotic Front stopped the Interahamwe, she returned home with her daughters to find her house an empty shell without doors or a roof. "I searched for help anywhere and everywhere," she says. "Our situation was desperate." Finally, the United Nations Office of the High Commissioner of Human Rights provided plastic sheeting to use as a roof. Until she began networking with other women, she felt alone, isolated and emptied out. "I was disgusted with myself and suicidal," she says. "By sharing my experience with other women, I have come to feel better about myself."

The Women for Women International-Rwanda sponsorship program gave her the funds necessary to get on her feet again. Today, she produces cassava and sweet potatoes and owns two cows and some goats. Being able to sustain herself and her children also increased Rosine's sense of self-worth.

"My late husband's uncle wanted to marry me," she says. "I did not want to marry him. Had I not had the means to support myself and my children or the self-confidence to stand up, I would have probably married him out of pressure. And this would have brought me a life of misery. I loved my husband, and I don't see myself with another man. I don't have that desire anymore."

AFTERWARD

Rosine and her two daughters survived the genocide. They survived near-drowning. Yet she says the psychological toll on her was so great that without the support of other women, she might have taken her own life.

BEAMING

Francine, a 33-year-old widow (left), sits in her home with Berra Kabarungi, director of Women for Women International. Francine is known for her radiant smile and optimism. She is shown (opposite) with her two daughters, one an orphan she adopted after the genocide.

Ababumba amatafari

Le 18.1.05	Le 13.1.05	Le 14.1.05	
1. Munyemana	Munyemana	Munyemana	1800
2. Nyangezi	Nyangezi	Nyangezi	1800
3. Abimana	Abimana	Mukaseku Ru	1800
4. Mutoni 600	Justin 600	ABIMANA	1800
5. Sibomana 600	Ruhinda	RUHINDA	1200
6. Mukasekuru	Mukasekuru	JUSTIN 400 AU nid	1600
106as			600
			600
			10600

THEY HACKED MY RIBS WITH A MACHETE AND LEFT ME TO DIE.

THAT NIGHT I SLEPT IN MY BLOOD,

THE BLOOD OF MY CHILDREN AND OF MY HUSBAND.

THINKING ABOUT THOSE IMAGES, MEDITATING ON MY PROBLEMS,

AT TIMES, I FIND IT DIFFICULT TO SLEEP AT NIGHT.

THE IMAGES COME TO ME OFTEN.

I AM LIVING IN THE SAME HOUSE, SURVIVING, AND COPING.

I HAD LOST APPRECIATION FOR LIFE AND MYSELF.

I WANTED TO DIE. I DIDN'T WANT TO TAKE ANY MEDICINE.

I FELT NO JOY. NOW THROUGH THE PROGRAM, THINGS ARE DIFFERENT.

I VALUE MYSELF.

—BEATA

A blackboard used in a women's training session in Kigali.

FRANCINE

The genocide puzzled many women when it started. It didn't make sense. Many Hutu and Tutsi had grown up as friends. They had married each other's brothers. They did not consider each other enemies. Their lives, in many ways, were lived as one. Then came the great "confusion," as Francine calls it. The Rwandan government started telling people that Tutsi were trying to take away the land of the Hutu.

The hatred that was created—that led to genocide—is not something that we will fully understand, ever," says Francine, the mother of two girls. "The Hutu were convinced that the Tutsi would take away their land. So they were driven to kill perceived enemies out of fear. It was confusing. It was just Rwandese killing other Rwandese for reasons that I don't believe we understood." Francine was 21 at the time, newly married, and pregnant. Her husband was a government soldier. When the killing started, suddenly it seemed, everyone was running in different directions. "I ran in confusion," she says. "I wanted to save my life and my baby."

She lost track of her husband and found herself swept along with waves of fleeing Rwandans across the border into the Democratic Republic of the Congo. She saw so much killing, she says, that she lost track of herself. Her mother, her father, and three brothers were killed. At one point, she believes she went insane. "I could not cope with what happened, and what I saw—so many losses," she says.

Like thousands of others fleeing the slaughter, she became a refugee in Congo. She was treated well, but missed her own country and longed to return. Finally, two years later, she went back to Rwanda only to find out that her husband had died somewhere in Congo. When she returned, she adopted a young orphan girl and struggled to raise her with her own young daughter.

"We had nothing, we were very poor," she says. "I had no resources to care for them, to feed them, and to send them to school. I knew that I was poor, but I did not know what to do about my poverty, you see. It is like a tree that was infected at the root."

Through participation in a gender-awareness program, she began meeting with other women, sharing experiences, and finding practical suggestions to increase her income. Francine is one of thousands of women who corresponded with Women for Women International sponsors in the United States, Europe, and other parts of the world. Sponsors also send monthly stipends to help women get back on their feet. "My relationship with my sponsor, Michelle, has opened a new world for me," she says. "I have talked to my sponsor about Rwanda, my husband, my evolution with the program. My sponsor has also talked to me about her life…. That relationship has contributed to changing some of my perceptions in life."

Today, she is the president of a local cooperative in her community that supports women and other members of the community. "I am always looking for ways to increase my knowledge and to improve my life," she says. "I am not bitter. I am hopeful for myself, my community, and my country. My life is a testimony to that optimism."

I AM NOT BITTER.

I AM HOPEFUL FOR MYSELF,

MY COMMUNITY,

AND MY COUNTRY.

—FRANCINE

Ku nuti yanjye nkunda cyane
Catherine

Ikirenze kubandikira nagirango mbaboke amakuru
yanyu ayanjye yo ni meza nuko bisazue ubungubu
imvura iraguwa imbogazaku zirera narubu kanjecye
nashe me shefut nuko muwanyakiriye nanjye narabakunze
cyane kandi nishemiye ifabo muwanyoherereje
ubungubu ndakora nfite aboha batatu umwana
umwe yiga muri sagenderi mu wa mbere arigo
numuhanga afite imyaka 14 umukuru afite imyaka
18 izi ue mfuro yanjye umuto yiga muri gari diyeni
abandi 2 umwe yiga 4 pirimeri undi 3 pirimeri
imfura ue kuko yabuze ishuri yiga umukanishi
nanjye uborerianye kyine ariko murophasha nago
ariawye nye nyine kuko munrera inkuhgo
ubu nanjye ndakolindo cyone nifujakiemenya
amakuru yanyu munrye muyangezaho nanjye
nzanza nyabagezaho nanjye naro
ndabakuhda

TO MY DEAREST CATHERINE,

HOW ARE YOU DOING? HERE IN RWANDA WE ARE ALSO FINE.

NOW WE ARE IN THE RAINY SEASON. IT'S COLD IN THE NIGHTS,

AND WE ARE GROWING MANY VEGETABLES NOW.

I WAS VERY HAPPY TO KNOW THAT YOU ACCEPTED ME, AND I LOVE YOU SO MUCH.

THANK YOU FOR YOUR PICTURE. MYSELF, I HAVE FIVE CHILDREN.

MY OLDEST IS 18 YEARS OLD, AND HE IS STUDYING MECHANICS, THE SECOND ONE IS

IN SECONDARY SCHOOL, HE IS 14 YEARS AND VERY BRIGHT.

THE OTHERS ARE IN PRIMARY SCHOOL, THIRD AND SECOND GRADE, AND MY LAST ONE IS IN

KINDERGARTEN. I HAVE MANAGED TO PUT THEM IN SCHOOL WITH YOUR HELP

THAT YOU HAVE BEEN SENDING ME. I REALLY WOULD LIKE TO HEAR FROM YOU, TOO,

AND AM SO GLAD TO HAVE MET YOU. I LOVE YOU VERY MUCH, I LEAVE IT FOR NOW.

WE THANK YOU FOR THE LOVE YOU'VE SHOWN US.

—CHRISTINE

A letter from Christine of Rwanda to her sponsor.

Dorothy and her mother (above) and (opposite)
with three of her children and her mother.

I WANT TO MAKE SURE
THAT MY CHILDREN CONTINUE WITH
THEIR EDUCATION, FOR I WAS
NOT ABLE TO CONTINUE WITH MINE,
AND I THINK EDUCATION
IS THE SALVATION OF THE POOR.

—DOROTHY

THIS LIFE IS A BATTLE

AND A VERY DIFFICULT

DILEMMA FOR ME.

AS I WORRY ABOUT DYING

BEFORE BOBETTE,

I ALSO WORRY ABOUT HER

DYING BEFORE ME.

WHO WILL CARE FOR HER,

IF I AM NOT AROUND?

—MARIE CLAIRE

MARIE CLAIRE

She was pregnant with her third child when Marie Claire went to the clinic for a routine prenatal checkup, and the doctor told her she was HIV-positive.

"I was alone when I found out," she says. "I was devastated and angry, angry that this could happen to me. I could not believe that it was me. I have never been with another man except for my husband; I could not understand how I could be sick with this virus."

HIV comes home to haunt women and children, especially in Africa when war sends soldiers off to battle. Marie Claire brought her husband in for testing, and it turned out he was positive. Ultimately, he accepted responsibility and realized he would have to live with the knowledge that he was the cause of their illness. But the greatest tragedy, they found out, was that Marie Claire had already passed on the virus to their second child, a little girl named Bobette, through her breast milk. When she gave birth to her third child, she did not breastfeed, and the baby is healthy.

"Surviving the genocide, I did not believe that living with HIV/AIDS would be my fate," she says. "But I have to live with the consequences of our relationship. It doesn't help to be angry now. He is dying. We are dying. If I am angry, I will be paralyzed. There is no time for me to be angry. There is too much to do."

Today she cares for Bobette, her husband, and herself while her eldest child and her baby live with her parents. Her husband's disease has progressed rapidly. "I do not know how much longer my husband has on Earth," she says. As for the little girl, her body is small and frail—"too weak to handle all of this."

Of the three infected family members, Marie Claire is the strongest. She cultivates some land with other women in her community. A stipend from a monthly sponsor helps her purchase food and medicine for her family. She is also active in her community, where she is helping to promote HIV/AIDS education. In particular, she is teaching women about the importance of early testing and ways HIV-positive women can safeguard their unborn babies.

"I have to go on living, despite knowing that death is a certainty," she says with resolve. "Death is a certainty for all of us. My fate is just clearer."

*Bobette (opposite),
dressed up to have her picture
taken, holds a lily.
Marie Claire, her husband,
and her daughter, Bobette
(left), all HIV-positive,
pose for a family portrait.*

NTARAMA CHURCH

*The Catholic church where thousands of Tutsi
sought refuge still bears witness to
their slaughter in 1994. Rows of skulls show
machete hack marks. Bones
and scraps of clothing are scattered
where pews once stood.*

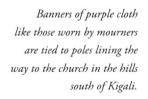

Banners of purple cloth like those worn by mourners are tied to poles lining the way to the church in the hills south of Kigali.

DYING TO LIVE

It is a small church, too small for 5,000 people to gather, let alone die. In this overwhelmingly Christian country, Tutsi were told by government officials that they could find safety in the churches that dot the hilltops across Rwanda.

"We did not know why we were brought to the church to be slaughtered," says Jemince, 40. The *Interahamwe*—a term in the Kinyarwanda language that means "those who attack together"—surrounded the church and attacked. In the chaos, she was separated from her family. Her other children disappeared. She was left alone with her nine-month-old baby strapped to her back.

"People were falling over me," Jemince says. "I was soaked in blood. There were dead bodies and blood everywhere…but my little boy did not cry. It was as if he knew keeping silent meant his life. For certain, if he had cried they would have looked for the noise, and they would have killed us right away."

So they lay there, amid the bodies, Jemince and her baby pretending together to be dead in order to survive.

The genocide had gone on for nearly 100 days by this time. Rebel troops were approaching—Jemince could hear the shots—and it seemed to her that the Interahamwe moved about faster, trying to kill as many people as possible before their time was up. They methodically checked each of the bodies in the church, one by one, to finish off anyone who remained alive. That was when they found her and the child, still quiet, and took them outside with others to kill.

Suddenly, shots rang out nearby and the approach of rebel forces could be heard. People scattered. She ran with her baby. Later, she found two of her other five children. But she lost her husband, three children, her mother, and virtually all her relatives in the massacre. She adopted three orphans.

"Those of us who adopted orphans did so with little or no means to care for ourselves and our own surviving children," she says. "But we had no choice. There were too many children left orphaned by the genocide. It was not possible to sit on the side and do nothing."

Today, the church is more of a memorial than a museum. Battered skulls and bone fragments lie among clothing and common utensils brought to this place by victims who assumed they would need them to cook or wash. When the church became a museum, it was opened first to survivors. People swooned. There are exhibits dedicated to murdered children. There is a collection of machetes and garden tools that were used to carry out the killings.

There are also notes, memoirs left by visitors, and swaths of purple cloth tied to a fence around the partly destroyed old church. Purple is the color of mourning. "Never again," says graffiti scribbled onto walls in English, French, and Kinyarwanda.

VIRUNGA MOUNTAINS

Rwanda, dotted with small farms,
is the most densely populated nation in Africa.
The Virunga range of volcanoes encompassing
a branch of the Great Rift Valley
is the site of endangered animal preserves.
It is through this range that many refugees from
Rwanda escaped genocide—
pouring into the Democratic Republic
of the Congo—and later returned
home to rebuild.

ACKNOWLEDGMENTS

This book was a labor of love and a reflection of the importance of hearing what women have to say about war and peace. This project was a dream of Women for Women International, but it took the energy and commitment of many women to make it a reality.

I am grateful for photo editor Deb Feingold, who helped us identify our talented photographers and select their incredible photos for the book. Special thanks and gratitude to photographers Sylvia Plachy, Susan Meiselas, and Lekha Singh for generously volunteering their time and taking the risks associated with traveling to conflict or post-conflict zones; it was an honor and privilege to work with and learn from their insights.

Thanks to Donna Schinderman for her inspiration early on in the project. And, of course, we could not have executed the project without the generous contribution from our anonymous donor.

We are grateful to our agent Martha Kaplan, who volunteered huge numbers of hours to help us develop a book proposal and who undertook the negotiations. Special thanks to our publisher, National Geographic, and particularly to Barbara Brownell Grogan for her enthusiasm and belief in the book. Yo Cuomo not only made the ideas and images come through in the most beautiful ways, but her free spirit made working with her a pleasure. We are thankful to the book's editor, Laurie Becklund, whose artistic writing helps ensure that women's voices come through clear and strong.

Thanks also to Women for Women International's own team, especially to Karen Sherman, COO of Women for Women International and our executive producer, whose vision, time, and articulation of this project made it possible. Longtime friend and colleague Mary Daly, a visionary creative producer, helped translate vision into reality by introducing us to almost everyone involved. I am also thankful to Corey Oser for her research and editorial assistance, to Tobey Goldfarb and Board member Susan Vitka for their input on the introduction, and finally to Ricki Weisberg for her incredible work in editing, research, information-gathering, and coordination of this project.

My gratitude also to our colleagues in the field: Sweeta Noori, Farida Faqqiri, Yalda Seddiqi, and Saida Maqsudi in Afghanistan;

Berra Kabarungi in Rwanda; Natasha Gartner, Betsabe Paez, Luz Angela Olaya, and Clemencia Guarnizo in Colombia; Seida Saric, Alma Budakovic, Amira Karcic, Renata Raus, Alma Hodzic, Jasmina Cengic, Amna Imamovic, Varja Djurovic, Mirela Avdic, Zijada Suvalija, Anisa Posao, Dienne Miller, Ajsa Sacic, Senija Frzina, Mirela Ahmetovic, Amra Krvavac, Razija Bosnjak, and Divnaa Đokic in Bosnia and Herzegovina; and Karak Mayik Nyok in Sudan for their incredible work in unstable environments, for introducing us to these women, and for their editorial assistance. Special thanks to Judithe Registre for her role in making the Rwanda, Democratic Republic of the Congo and Sudan chapters possible.

Last but definitely not least, I am in gratitude to a great teacher and woman, Alice Walker, for her support of this book and of Women for Women International's work and mission. I feel a huge sense of privilege, honor, and humility working with the great women featured in this book and those who helped make it possible. They are, indeed, women creating change in the world.

NOW I PARTICIPATE IN MEETINGS WITH OUR NATION'S MOST IMPORTANT PEOPLE LIKE JOURNALISTS, MAYORS.... I EVEN PARTICIPATED IN A SENATORS' MEETING ONCE. AFTER ATTENDING A MEETING OUTSIDE MY VILLAGE, I CAME BACK AND ORGANIZED MY FELLOW VILLAGEMATES' MEETING.

—CECILE
from Rwanda

STRONGER WOMEN

BUILD STRONGER

NATIONS.

—ZAINAB SALBI

CONTRIBUTORS

Susan Meiselas is a documentary photographer, known for her work in conflict zones. A member of Magnum Photos since 1976, Meiselas's work has appeared in publications worldwide. Her books include: *Carnival Strippers; Nicaragua; El Salvador: The Work of 30 Photographers; Chile from Within; Kurdistan: In the Shadow of History;* and *Encounters with the Dani.* A 1992 MacArthur Fellow, she has received awards including the Leica Award for Excellence, Maria Moors Cabot Award, and the Cornell Capa Infinity Award.

Sylvia Plachy's body of work spans four decades, appearing in the *Village Voice,* the *New York Times,* the *New Yorker,* and many other publications. A graduate of the Pratt Institute, she is the recipient of honors including the Guggenheim Fellowship and the Women In Photography International's Lucie Award. The most recent of her four books, *Self Portrait with Cows Going Home* (Aperture), is her own story of Eastern Europe, which she fled with her parents during the Hungarian Revolution in 1956. Her work appears in museums and collections worldwide.

Lekha Singh uses photography to introduce marginalized and socially excluded citizens of the world. She works in countries such as Kenya, Vietnam, Cambodia, China, Mexico, and her native India. Her photographs were exhibited in New York at the National Arts Club and shown at the 2004 Paralympics in Athens.

Laurie Becklund is a bilingual journalist (Spanish/English), author, and independent editor. A former *Los Angeles Times* staff writer, she has explored subjects ranging from slumlords and Salvadoran death squads to technology, winning awards for writing and investigative reporting and a share of a staff Pulitzer Prize. She is co-author of three bestselling books: *SWOOSH: The Story of Nike and the Men Who Played There; Go Toward the Light;* and (with Zainab Salbi) *Between Two Worlds: Escape from Tyranny: Growing Up in the Shadow of Saddam.*

Yolanda Cuomo Design has produced for over 20 years a wide range of projects that demonstrate the firm's passion and skill, crafting striking visual solutions that merge words with images. Projects include: book and exhibition design for *Diane Arbus Revelations; New York, September 11 by Magnum Photographers; Farewell to Bosnia,* a book of photographs by Gilles Peress; *Pre Pop Warhol;* and *Here is New York: A Democracy of Photographs.* Yolanda Cuomo Design's work has been honored with several industry awards, including, most recently the Infinity award, and the 2004 National Magazine Award in the category of General

Excellence from the American Society of Magazine Editors (ASME) for the art direction of *Aperture* magazine.

Deborah Feingold is best known for portraits of high-profile subjects ranging from Nobel Laureate Desmond Tutu and Madonna to the Rolling Stones. Over the past 15 years she has served as a contract photographer to *Rolling Stone, US Weekly,* and *People* magazine. Feingold often photographs authors for book jackets. She has published two books of her own photographs and is a contributor to many collections. She has won numerous awards, including from the Society of Publication Designers and the Art Directors Clubs of New York and Boston. She lives in New York City with her 12-year-old daughter.

Zainab Salbi is the author of *Between Two Worlds: Escape from Tyranny: Growing Up in the Shadow of Saddam* and the founder of Women for Women International. She frequently speaks to the media and international audiences about women in post-conflict societies, which includes several appearances on the *Oprah Winfrey Show*. She is the recipient of the 2005 Forbes Trailblazer Award, was named "Innovator of the Month" by *Time* magazine, and was honored by President Bill Clinton for her humanitarian work.

Alice Walker won the Pulitzer Prize and the American Book Award for her third novel, *The Color Purple,* which was made into an internationally popular film and is now being performed as a Broadway musical. She is the author of numerous best-selling novels, several collections of short stories, essays, and poems, as well as children's books.

THE OTHER SIDE OF WAR
Zainab Salbi

Published by the National Geographic Society
John M. Fahey, Jr., President and Chief Executive Officer
Gilbert M. Grosvenor, Chairman of the Board
Nina D. Hoffman, Executive Vice President;
President, Books and School Publishing

Prepared by the Book Division
Kevin Mulroy, Senior Vice President and Publisher
Kristin Hanneman, Illustrations Director
Marianne R. Koszorus, Design Director

Barbara Brownell Grogan, Executive Editor
Elizabeth Newhouse, Director of Travel Publishing
Leah Bendavid-Val, Director of Photography Publishing
Carl Mehler, Director of Maps

Staff for this Book
Karin Kinney, Editor
Matt Chwastyk, Thomas L. Gray, and
Mapping Specialists, Map Research and Production
Lauren Pruneski, Assistant Editor
Lewis Bassford, Production Project Manager
Abby Lepold, Illustrations Specialist
Cameron Zotter, Design Assistant

Rebecca Hinds, Managing Editor
Gary Colbert, Production Director

Book Design, Yolanda Cuomo Design, NYC
Kristi Norgaard, Design Associate

Manufacturing and Quality Management
Christopher A. Liedel, Chief Financial Officer
Phillip L. Schlosser, Vice President
John T. Dunn, Technical Director
Vincent P. Ryan, Director
Chris Brown, Director
Maryclare Tracy, Manager

Founded in 1888, the National Geographic Society is one of the largest nonprofit scientific and educational organizations in the world.

It reaches more than 285 million people worldwide each month through its official journal, NATIONAL GEOGRAPHIC, and its four other magazines; the National Geographic Channel; television documentaries; radio programs; films; books; videos and DVDs; maps; and interactive media. National Geographic has funded more than 8,000 scientific research projects and supports an education program combating geographic illiteracy.

For more information, please call
1-800-NGS LINE (647-5463)
or write to the following address:

National Geographic Society
1145 17th Street N.W.
Washington, D.C. 20036-4688 U.S.A.

Log on to nationalgeographic.com;
AOL Keyword: NatGeo.

For information about special discounts
for bulk purchases, please contact
National Geographic Books Special Sales:
ngspecsales@ngs.org

Library of Congress Cataloging-in-Publication Data available upon request.
ISBN-10: 0-7922-6211-5
ISBN-13: 978-0-7922-6211-4